Tales of Forgotten Kent

Malcolm Horton

The History Press

Front cover image credit: The Estate of the late Dennis Flanders RWS RBA.

First published 2024

The History Press
97 St George's Place, Cheltenham,
Gloucestershire, GL50 3QB
www.thehistorypress.co.uk

British Library Cataloguing in Publication Data.
A catalogue record for this book is available from the British Library.

ISBN 978 1 80399 746 9

Typesetting and origination by The History Press
Printed and bound in Great Britain by TJ Books Limited, Padstow, Cornwall.

MIX
Paper | Supporting responsible forestry
FSC® C013056

Trees for Life

Contents

Acknowledgements

I would particularly like to thank the following:

The Estate of the late Dennis Flanders RWS RBA for the permission to use the two paintings featured in Chapter 2 and painting in Chapter 5.

Dennis Roxby Bott for his painting in Chapter 2.

Jane Carpanini RWS RWE for permission to use the two paintings in Chapter 4.

David Burke, present owner of Ripley Court, for providing a photograph of his famous dwelling in Chapter 6.

James Buss, Mine Host and owner of the Dering Arms for the last 35 years, for supplying information about the Dering Hunting Lodge.

Introduction

This collection of twenty-two essays was written mainly for *Bygone Kent*, with others appearing in *This England*, *Kent Life* and the late lamented *Journal of Kent History*. The criteria for these essays were legend, folklore, people and events that have largely been neglected by historians, but all are part of Kent's rich tapestry associated with its unique position as the gateway to England, going back to early Stone-Age settlers 400,000 years ago. It was where, in 55 BC, Julius Caesar first set foot on English soil.

St Augustine, who brought Christianity to England in AD 597, landed at Ebbsfleet on the Isle of Thanet. And on that same island, St Mildred, the second abbess, gave her name to Minster Abbey, which her mother, Princess Domneva established in AD 670 in recompense for the murder of her two princely brothers by King Egbert of Kent's evil counsellor, Thurnor, who met a fitting end when the ground opened up and swallowed him. Minster then became the capital of Thanet.

The Jutes, part of the Anglo-Saxon influx, first established themselves in Kent, and it was two early Anglo-Saxon tribes who divided Kent, east and west of the River Medway, and gave rise to the soubriquets 'Men of Kent', born east of the Medway, and 'Kentish Man' to those born west of the Medway.

Who would have thought that the cradle of British aviation was the unfashionable Isle of Sheppey? Or that the greatest technological change in printing, computer-assisted typesetting, first took place in Europe in the small town of Westerham in 1965, just a stone's throw from Winston Churchill's home at Chartwell, and just a few miles from where the father of British printing, William Caxton, was born in the Weald – possibly Tenterden or Hadlow – in 1450?

It also seems hard to imagine that the Weald of Kent was, in the sixteenth century, the centre of the English iron-smelting industry, fuelled by charcoal from the abundant oak trees and local iron ore deposits. It only moved to the coal-producing areas of south Wales and the north of England in the seventeenth century.

It seems unbelievable that the first and only recognised American royal princess, Pocahontas, is buried in Gravesend or that the poet who wrote the first English sonnet was not Shakespeare but Sir Thomas Wyatt the Elder, a reputed lover of Anne Boleyn, from Allington Castle near Maidstone. Also revealed is the connection in the village of Bridge, near Canterbury, between James Bond, a dashing 1920s motor-racing driver, Count Louis Zborowski, and the children's novel *Chitty Chitty Bang Bang*.

According to the writer H.E. Bates, Kent was one of the healthiest parts of England in which to live because it was rich in iodine because Kent is practically an island, surrounded by the sea and the rivers Thames and Medway.

The Kent countryside is defined by two parallel ridges that traverse the county from west to east, the chalk North Downs (home to the Pilgrims Way) and the sandstone Greensand Ridge. South of these two promontories is the clay Weald of Kent, once richly forested by oak trees and home to the thirty-four 'den' hamlets – Tenterden, Benenden, Bethersden, Biddenden and Smarden, among others. Dens were originally clearings where pigs and boars could winter and feed off the acorns from the abundant oak trees.

It was these special characteristics, defined by the writer E.H. Thomas as the 'South Country', which were the catalysts that persuaded writer and poet H.E. Bates to forsake his native Rushden, in Northamptonshire, and move to Little Chart, near Pluckley, and to immortalise Kent in his books *A Moment in Time*, *Down by the River* and his most famous Kent evocation, *The Darling Buds of May*. This book is a celebration of this wonderful county, which has been home to my family (most likely of Jutish origin) for over 500 years.

Finally, for those who wish to learn more of Kent and its customs, folklore and history, I would heartily recommend Sir Charles Igglesden's thirty-five volumes of *A Saunter Through Kent with Pen and Pencil*, written between 1899 and 1946 and covering 242 of Kent's villages.

1

Selling's Unique Mesolithic Past, 5,000 BC

The first part of this essay is an extract from Sir Charles Igglesden's articles from the *Kentish Express,* published between 18 December 1942 and 15 January 1943, although his visit must have been made earlier in the war because he is refers to boughs being heavily laden with fruit. Strict press censorship in the early part of the war delayed publication until censorship was eased in late 1942. He was clearly a man on a mission to find the so-called Pulpit and other ancient artefacts for which the Perry Wood area of Selling was famous.

The second part of the essay is a follow-up visit I made in 2023 to see how Selling had changed since Igglesden's visit and whether more ancient relics had been discovered in the eighty years since his visit.

Charles Igglesden's Visit to Selling, *c.* 1942

Try to find a little village among the hills of north-east Kent named Selling. In these winding lanes, happily, they have been spared the formal main road that normally kills scenery – you can lose yourself in normal times, but war was on, I tried to find Selling without any sign-post to guide me. But what a glorious bit of countryside when you reach the busiest part of the village, with its inn, the White Lion, newly built on the site of an older one; its couple of general shops and a long low red brick building that originally did service as a workhouse, but is now converted into a row of cottages. And that's all I could find in the so-called Street. Facing the end of the road is one of the entrances to the park, the seat of Earl Sondes.

But alongside the roads can be glimpsed old-world residences and farmsteads standing isolated amid all sorts of trees a wealth of orchards and, now and again, a hop garden. But hops are no longer grown in the same abundance as they were, before the powers-that-be ruthlessly cut down the acreage in all parts of England. There is one fine stack of oast-houses. But if several hop gardens have gone, the cherry orchards remain. Acres of them.

When I was in their midst with heavily laden boughs with ripening fruit, I and my friends became good specimens of human beings whose fate is to have their mouths water at the thought of joys to come. For we were a week too early to taste the full flavoured fruit and watch the fruit gathering in the orchards from Faversham and adjacent places. One picture was worth remembering – a Land Girl in a green jersey at the top of a ladder picking early cherries. A sign of the times when women were doing their bit for England, smiling uncomplaining.

In Domesday, Selling is spelt Sellinge and the confusion of this village with Sellinge near Hythe led to many disputes, even of a legal character. One testator left property in 'Sellinge, Kent', and one of his nephews who lived in Selling claimed it, while the other also argued that he was the beneficiary as his uncle also had property in Sellinge. The Selling man won and incidentally became bankrupt; for law costs were as heavy in the seventeenth century as they are today. And here is another case of the clash of names. Sellinge claims to be the birth place of William Selling, a notable prior of Christ Church Canterbury, where he was buried in 1494. Most old biographies give Selling priority in its claim to call the learned prior as one of its famous sons. Before he became prior, he was a monk and is described by one of his biographies as being possessed of learning and wisdom.

The people of Selling are proud of their Pulpit, a mound in the heart of the woods. 'How do I get to it?' I asked. The reply of my guide was probably familiar to the native, but it was confusing to hear that turning sometimes to the right and sometimes to the left, many of them, would bring me to the Rose. Yes; there was the inn staring me in the face, and in front – it was not yet opening time – was a group of young khaki-clad soldiers, some lounging against it, some sprawling on the dusty roadside, all very cheerful, all very sun-burnt. But if you wish to glean the whereabouts of any place nowadays, don't ask a member of His Majesty's Forces for good reason – he will probably know the direction and, if he does, regulations very properly forbid him to give the information.

I was in search of something connected with war – not Sir Thomas Wyatt's rebellion, although a few of the youth of the district joined the forces of that ill-fated knight. No, what I intended to search for was some ancient fortification vaguely referred to by many Kent historians without giving any defaults as to position.

That the Pulpit had some connection with the ancient camp I was convinced, so I must find it first and then take my bearings. I followed the simple method of asking two small girls where the Pulpit was. They pointed to a fine display of small trees, the clump rising to a considerable height. 'How do I get there?' I asked. 'I dunno' one replied and the other shook her head till a truant lock of curls hung over her eyes. But it was not the information they gave but their happy smiles that won the pennies. And their waving hands as they went away was a cheery sight and a friendly gesture that would have won them another copper had they not been so far away.

And then along the lane came a figure in khaki breeches and jersey with swinging gait. Brown her face, delightful her features, bright her eyes – a picture of the type of health that only the countryside could give. I should have liked to be inquisitive – what in peace time was the sort of air she breathed. Was it in a close street and a stuffy office which meant a pale face and less physical vigour and enjoyment? I do not know but she made me proud of those Land Girls who are helping us to win the war. She knew where the Pulpit was and pointed to the same spot selected by my two little schoolgirl friends. And she walked on with the same easy gait not withstanding a long day's work on the land. Her parting smile was worth ever more attraction than the smiles of my little friends – but you don't give pennies to Land Girls.

Then along came a perfect specimen of the race that has given rural England the foremost place in the agricultural world. He may have been sixty or seventy, but by his walk he was nearer the age of the townsmen of fifty. While whiskered, he was with a healthy colouring to a face that would probably retain the brownish tint throughout the snow falls and frost of winter; that friendly good-natured smile and lazy drawl with a true Kentish accent. In reply to my question 'Where was the Pulpit?' his eyes lit up with pride, for as I have said before, the Selling people think much of their possession, though few, methinks, know that in the nearby wide are the remains of an ancient camp.

Close to the inn is a footpath or narrow lane leading to a clump of trees you have seen from the road. One side is obviously banked up and this is part of the scarp of the ancient earth-work. Yes, certainly very ancient. But antiquaries disagree as to its date – Saxon, Danish or Roman. There is no reason why it should not date back to pre-Roman times, for when the Germans invaded Britain during the fifth century they came in three distinct batches at different times. The earliest arrivals were the Jutes and they settled in the south-east and for the most part in Kent. The Romans probably discovered the old site and selected it as a summer camp and added to its defensive strength. It is impossible to trace any but part of the old fortress, but careful inspection brings to light undulating ground with a distinct earth wall facing the level country to the south-east.

The so-called Pulpit was a mound erected as an observation post which in extremity the defences would find useful for a last stand against an enemy that had broken through the trenches. On this mound, a rough wooden structure was erected in the last century and it is recorded that preachers of religion addressed the people from this spot. Even Courtenay, the Kent fanatic who was eventually shot in Blean Woods, used this mound as a platform when addressing his followers. Now-a-days the spot is a happy rendezvous for picnic parties and in peace time vehicles by the dozen were drawn up in a roadway close by. One feature of Shottenden Hill – the present local name for it – is the number of springs and running water which would emphasise its value as a camp.

In several parts of Selling stone implements of early English have been dug up. On one occasion an old antiquary was walking in a wood when he saw two boys playing with what they probably thought were ordinary stones, but they were in fact, fine Palaeolithic specimens and are now in the British Museum. Now hidden by a clump of trees is an ancient tumulus, about half a mile north of the Pulpit. I wonder what old Roman warrior lies buried there. Thus, this quiet and simple little Kentish village of Selling has a history dating back many centuries.

Selling Revisited, 2018

Igglesden spent much time trying to find the old archaeological workings and the Pulpit. The common denominator geographically is the Rose & Crown hostelry, to the north of which is the Perry Wood earthworks which contain the remains of ancient Mesolithic (10,000–5,000 BC) settlements. Relics from the late Stone Age to Iron Age periods have been discovered, such as flint axes and pottery. In the 1970s, Swale Borough Council bought Perry Woods from Corpus Christi College Oxford as a public amenity. In 2008, the Mid-Kent Downs Partnership became involved, and excavations in Perry Wood have since taken place. The mound site of the earthworks, Windmill Hill, was once occupied by a post windmill that was constructed in 1596 and was still in use until the early twentieth century.

South of the Rose and Crown, the woods are more properly known as Conduit Woods and this contains the Pulpit, from which, as Igglesden explains, great orators have preached. It stands 504ft above sea level and affords spectacular views over the Weald of Kent. Its wooden structure has been replaced many times.

It was while examining the Pulpit in June 2023 that I experienced an Igglesden moment. A local senior citizen was with a small boy, scrabbling around assiduously examining stones. The old man was explaining to his grandson that he might find stone implements from a bygone age. Engaging him in conversation, he told me that thirty years before he had found a stone flint axe that he took to the British Museum. He assured me that they had

The Rose and Crown.

The Pulpit.

The White Lion.

told him that it was from the Palaeolithic period (500,000 years old). He may have got that wrong – more like Mesolithic – but, nevertheless, a wonderful discovery, and worth an afternoon out to distract bored grandchildren.

One major change since Igglesden's visit: Selling Court is no more. It was pulled down in the 1960s, and together with the Earl of Sonde's Park, is now an attractive, beautifully landscaped, executive-style housing estate. Rhodes Court, however, has been tastefully restored and is still home to the Gaskain family.

Perry Woods also contains the Bandstand, which is also known as the Drawing Room and is so named because Salvation Army bands once played here, and teas were served. The whole area is now served by three public car parks, such is its popularity as a social amenity, with woodland walks all year round.

There is an excellent circular walk from Selling car park that takes in the two special woodland areas as well as being served by two excellent hostelries at either end (the other one is the White Lion, The Street, Selling). And there's always a chance you might find a stone hand tool from the Mesolithic period and retire to either pub to discuss its provenance.

2

The Oldest School in Britain, AD 597

It is now generally accepted that King's Canterbury is the oldest school in Britain. The distinguished historian A.F. Leach, after exhaustive research and at first proclaiming St Peter's, York, as the oldest, finally concluded that the King's Canterbury was an even earlier foundation.

He based this judgement on the fact that each cathedral had within its precincts a school. Church services were in Latin, and so it was necessary to teach the converts the Latin tongue – hence the need for a school. Therefore, the oldest cathedral – Canterbury – must, by definition, contain the oldest school. King's Canterbury can trace its origins back to about AD 597, when Augustine founded the cathedral. Based on A.F. Leach's reasoning, King's School, Rochester, would rank as the second-oldest school in Britain, with the appointment of Justus to the See of Rochester by Augustine in AD 604.

Further weight is given to Canterbury's claim to be the oldest by a statement made by the Venerable Bede of Jarrow (*c.* AD 673–735), Britain's early medieval historian. He wrote in AD 631, 'Sigbert presided over the Kingdom of East Anglia [*c.* AD 629–634] and founded a school with the assistance of Bishop Felix whom he had got from Canterbury and who in turn appointed ushers and masters after the custom of the Kentish folk.'

King's owes its name to Henry VIII. When he abolished St Augustine's Monastery, he re-endowed the school in 1541 and continuity was maintained by reappointing the same headmaster. At this time, the same re-endowment process and change in nomenclature was taking place in the other 'new' king's

St Augustine Great Gate. (Painting by Dennis Roxby Bott)

schools throughout England. Henry VIII also provided King's Canterbury with new statutes by which the school was to consist of '50 poor boys who were destitute and were to be maintained by the church'.

The chief purpose of cathedral schools such as Canterbury was to teach Latin, so they became known as grammar schools. Additionally, the school admitted eight choristers, who attended the song school for a less-demanding education than the grammar school. However, the choristers were allowed to sit together with grammar schoolboys at one table and both were allowed *2d* a week for 'commons' (food).

The King's School is inextricably entwined with the towering presence of the great cathedral and its associated buildings, which formed a quadrangle around the Mint Yard within the cathedral precincts. It remained confined in this way until 1976 when St Augustine's Abbey, which is outside the city walls, was acquired.

Connecting the school from its Green Court to the cathedral buildings is the Dark Entry, a passageway passing through Prior Selling's fifteenth-century gateway. According to a school legend made popular by Richard Barham in his *Ingoldsby Legends*, the passage is haunted by the ghost of Nell Cook. She was a servant girl to an elderly canon and became annoyed when he engaged in an affair. When the canon and his lover both died from poisoned food, the finger of suspicion pointed at Nell. Her punishment was to be buried alive under the flagstones that pave the Dark Entry. Her ghost walks the area, particularly on a Friday evening …

The Norman Staircase. (Painting by Dennis Flanders)

Speech Day in 1956. (Painting by Dennis Flanders)

The Ingoldsby Legends were published in 1837 and were very popular throughout the nineteenth century. The canon's lover was said to be his niece, but Nell had her doubts:

> Now welcome dearest niece
> come lay thy mantle by
> The canon kissed her ruby lips
> he had a merry eye
> But Nell Cook askew did look
> it came into her mind
> They were a little less than kin
> and rather more than kind

It is said that anyone unfortunate enough to see the ghost of Nell Cook will die soon after. The Dark Entry can be seen in Dennis Flanders's painting of the 1956 'Speech Day Garden Party'. It is to the left of the enormous marquee in the centre of the painting.

Perhaps the most famous building on the cathedral site is the Norman staircase that leads up to the Old School Room and dates from 1150. This is shown in Dennis Flanders's second painting of the school, completed in 1991, which was commissioned by the headmaster, Canon Anthony Phillips. He was keen to include female pupils in the painting to demonstrate the school's new status as fully co-educational, although girls had been admitted to the sixth form since 1972.

King's School's most influential headmaster was F.J. Shirley, who, during the period 1935–62, transformed the school from a minor and nearly bankrupt institution into a truly great school. He had initiated extensive rebuilding, including a school hall, deemed essential to any self-respecting headmaster. Before his appointment, he had written to Dr Hewlett Johnson, famous as the 'Red Dean', pointing out the deficiencies of the school. Despite what might have been perceived as temerity, he was appointed headmaster. He made good the deficiencies and, when he left twenty-seven years later, finances were sound, and numbers had increased from 200 to 500. Today, the number of pupils is more than 800.

Given that the origin of King's Canterbury was in the education of fifty poor boys, how did it then become a 'public school', with all its connotations of education for the rich and privileged? Archbishop Cranmer was responsible for this fundamental change in emphasis when he decreed in the early sixteenth century, 'If a gentleman's son be apt for learning, let him be admitted'. Thus began the usage of the 'public school' term. The fact that Mammon took over and led to the total domination of fee-paying students led to the elitist appellation being applied to the term 'public school'. This process was repeated in all schools throughout the country and so they became the province of the rich and privileged. In recent times, these schools have become embarrassed by the elitist connotation and prefer to be known as 'independent schools', a less controversial appellation.

Undoubtedly, King's School's most famous alumnus is Christopher Marlowe (1564–93), the Elizabethan dramatist and poet, who was born in the same year as William Shakespeare and is thought to have been a great influence on his more famous contemporary. He died at age 29, murdered in a tavern in Deptford in mysterious circumstances – there is evidence that he was operating as a secret agent, working for Sir Thomas Walsingham's intelligence service. His most famous plays are *Tamburlaine*, *The Jew of Malta*, *Edward the Second* and *Dr Faustus*.

Marlowe was one of the first recipients of the two scholarships to Corpus Christi Cambridge, which Mathew Parker set up for King's School pupils when he was master of Corpus from 1544–53. In 1558, he became the second Protestant Archbishop of Canterbury. The scholarships continued until about 1990 and a representative of Corpus Christi still serves on King's School's board of governors.

Other distinguished alumni of King's include Thomas Linacre, who entered the school in 1472 and later in life founded the Royal College of Physicians, and William Harvey, who discovered the circulation of the blood in the seventeenth century. Additional old King's scholars include the writers Hugh Walpole and Somerset Maugham. The latter wrote *Of Human Bondage*, in which he seems to have hated his schooldays. However, he became a benefactor, endowing a scholarship for the sons of manual workers, and he also left his collection of books to the school. His ashes lie in the Galpin Garden, just outside the library.

3

The Legend of St Mildred of Minster-in-Thanet, AD 670

In the preface to Volume 5 of his *Saunters Through Kent with Pen and Pencil* series, published in 1903, Charles Igglesden informs us that a reader had rebuked him for including so much legend and superstition in his essays. The reader then went on to say that, otherwise, Igglesden's essays were quite the best topographical surveys of Kent since Hasted at the end of the eighteenth century.

Igglesden's reply was that legends and folklore were part of the very fabric of our history. In fact, Minster-in-Thanet, and more particularly, its patron St Mildred, is the perfect example of this contention, because legend is the very basis of Minster's existence. We have the legend of the arch-assasin, Thurnor; the legend of the founder of Minster Abbey, Princess Domneva; and the legend of Domneva's daughter, St Mildred, the patron saint of Minster, after whom the abbey is named.

Firstly, it must be appreciated that nowhere in England has witnessed so much destruction, plundering, murdering and bloodshed as the Isle of Thanet, which has been the entry point to southern Britain since very early times. Romans, Anglo-Saxons, Danish Vikings and the Normans all wreaked havoc on this northerly tip of Kent. But an invader of a different sort, the peaceful St Augustine, brought Christianity to England in AD 597 and landed on the Isle of Thanet. There he met the Anglo-Saxon King Aethelbert, who as a result, embraced the doctrine of Christianity. It is King Aethelbert's great-grandchildren who were responsible for the foundation of St Mildred's Abbey and Minster.

The present-day remains of St Mildred's Abbey, with the Norman tower on the far left and the new chapel on the right.

Thurnor's Leap is now a caravan park.

However, it was against a background of violence, so familiar to Thanet, that our story begins, in around AD 670 when Egbert was King of Kent. He had in his charge his two orphaned cousins, Aethelbert and Aethelred, who were treated like the young princes they were. This caused a great deal of jealousy on the part the weak king's evil counsellor, Thurnor, a true Dickensian-type character of the Uriah Heap variety. He advised Egbert that the young princes posed a threat to his rule and should be eliminated. This caused Egbert much anxiety. Thurnor took matters into his own hands and had the princes murdered.

The young princes' sister, Princess Domneva, sought recompense under the customary Saxon law of Weregild (blood money) from Egbert, who was greatly distressed at what had been done in his name. He readily agreed to grant a gift of land on Thanet, where Domneva could establish a priory.

It is the way the size of the land to be granted was determined that is unusual. Egbert agreed that it would be based on the amount of land that could be covered by Domneva's young deer (a hind) in one run. The extent of the hind's run caused great consternation to Thurnor, who tried to impede the hind. But miraculously, the ground opened up and swallowed the evil Thurnor in a place now called Thurnor's Leap, on the high ground of Mount Pleasant.

The first three abbesses. (Left to right: St Mildred, Princess Domneva and St Edburga.)

With the land granted to her, in AD 670 Domneva founded her priory on what is now the site of St Mary's Church. Meanwhile, her daughter Mildred was being educated at the Abbey of Chelles, near Paris. Here she would have learned the fine arts – Latin, scripture, poetry, etc. – in the company of other Saxon girls. When she returned to England, she joined her mother as a nun of St Mary's in Minster. In about AD 690, Domneva retired and St Theodore consecrated Mildred abbess.

Unfortunately, the Danish raids continued and on one famous occasion, they threw Mildred into a fiery oven. After some time, they opened the oven expecting to find a charred corpse but, lo and behold, the saintly Mildred emerged unscathed. The Danes fled, frightened by the miracle they had witnessed. It was these events that led to the founding of the abbey, the Minster of Thanet, and with it the status as the capital of the Isle of Thanet.

St Mildred and Minster Abbey's importance is given even more credence by a recently found charter dated AD 724 from the King of Kent, granting lands at Brentingsleag and on the Isle of Oxney, both in West Kent, for the grazing of cattle. As a result, Brentlingsleag became known as Tenterden, meaning 'Land granted for Thanet folk in a clearing in the Forest [den]'.

St Mildred died in around AD 725 and was succeeded by St Edburga. The story of Domneva looms so large in the legend of Minster that, to this day, the village sign contains as its motif Domneva's Hind.

In about AD 740, the community of nuns had grown to around seventy and they needed more space, so the third abbess, St Edburga, built a new convent in AD 741 on the present site of Minster Abbey, which is opposite St Mary's Church.

In about AD 840, the Danish Vikings burnt the abbey to the ground and it lay in ruin until 1027, when the Viking King Canute granted the abbey property to the Benedictine monks of Canterbury, and there it remained, despite desecration and reconstruction by the invading Normans, until 1538. At this date, Henry VIII dissolved the monasteries and Minster Abbey became a domestic dwelling named Minster Court.

This was famously owned from 1668 by the Earls of Conyngham, who were still lords of the manor at the time of Igglesden's visit in 1902. However, like a lot of landed gentry after the First World War, they were finding it difficult to manage financially, so they sold their Minster estate to Mr Charles and Mrs Lucie Senior in 1928, who in turn sold it in 1937 to Benedictine nuns from Bavaria, who were escaping from Nazi persecution. And so, after 400 years, once again Minster became a Benedictine foundation.

By Direction of Charles H. Senior, Esq.

The Oldest House in England, Minster Abbey, Thanet.

Between Sandwich and the North Foreland.

THE Ancient Abbey is of stone and is **reputed to be the oldest house in England,** the western wing being formed from the Nunnery built in the reign of Egbert. It contains 2 halls, 4 reception rooms, 14 bed and dressing rooms, 2 bath rooms. Company's **gas and water** are laid on, **main drainage**; Garages and stabling, 2 cottages, fine old manorial barn. Old-world gardens with spreading lawns, bowling green, tennis lawn, and park-like pasture; in all about **twelve acres.**

To be offered for Sale by Auction in the Hanover Square Estate Room on Tuesday, 24th September, 1935, at 2.30 p.m. (unless previously sold privately).

Solicitors :—Messrs. Fowell, Sayer and Thorold, Bank Plain, Norwich.

Auctioneers :—Messrs. Knight, Frank and Rutley, 20, Hanover Square, London, W.1.

The auction catalogue entry from 1935 when Mr and Mrs Senior put Minster Court up for sale.

An intriguing story exists about the circumstances surrounding the decision by Mr and Mrs Senior to sell Minster Court in 1935. It was initially offered for sale by auction as the 'oldest house in England' with fourteen bedrooms. It was withdrawn because of a dream Lucie Senior had one night in which an unknown monk told her that the property must return to the Church. This greatly unsettled her as she was of a sensitive disposition.

By complete coincidence, as if in answer to her dream, a monk, Dom Bede Winslow, from nearby St Augustine's Abbey in Ramsgate, contacted the Seniors and asked if he might be given time to seek a buyer from the monastic community. Because of her dream, Lucie persuaded her husband to follow this course of action, and so Minster Court was withdrawn from the auction.

Dom Bede began his search throughout Britain and Europe to find a monastic order that might be interested in purchasing Minster Court. That is how the Benedictine order of nuns from Bavaria came to settle in Minster in 1937. A fanciful story or fact? No one can be sure, but Igglesden, if he had been writing his essay now, would almost certainly have included it as one of his legends.

* * *

In 1987, there were two important events at the abbey which, at the time, were disasters, but in the end turned out to be fortune disguised. The first, in August 1987, was a great fire that engulfed the wooden chapel, razing it to the ground. And then, two months later, a hurricane swept across the south of England, destroying several ancient trees in the grounds of Minster Abbey. After six years of fundraising and the proceeds from the fire insurance, a phoenix literally arose from the ashes of the old chapel in the form of a beautiful new chapel, with an altar carved from one of the ancient trees that had been felled by the hurricane. In the end, it was a fitting tribute to mark fifty years since the refounding of Minster Abbey in 1937.

Nine nuns initially came from Bavaria, and they have been augmented by a further two. They live their simple life of prayer (seven services a day) and hard work, which involves working their farm, producing works of art and running a retreat for those who wish to spend time away from the hustle and bustle of everyday life. Conducted tours of the abbey take place every Saturday carried by the abbess, Mother Nikola. There is also a café and museum/ art gallery, Parkminster, which is run by volunteers and is very popular with the public.

New chapel interior, Minster Abbey.

4

Hempsted Park, Wealden: Home to a World-Famous School, 1086

In the early 1920s, due to an unprecedented demand for more and better public schools for girls, Miss Francis Dove, the dynamic founder and headmistress of Wycombe Abbey School, challenged members of her staff to start another school like her own 1896 foundation. Three of her staff – Miss Bird, Miss Hindle and Miss Sheldon – took up her challenge.

In July 1923, a furnished school was founded in Bickley, south London, and became the temporary home of the school until January 1924, when a permanent home was secured. Hempsted Park, a Victorian mansion set in 250 acres of Wealden countryside near the village of Benenden in Kent, was purchased from Lord Rothermere for £22,500. The school was named Benenden and not Hempsted Park School to avoid confusion with Hemel Hempstead in Hertfordshire.

The Hempsted Park Estate is of great historical interest, being mentioned in the Domesday Book as belonging to Bishop Odo, half-brother of William the Conqueror. In 1388, Richard II granted Hempsted Park to William de Guldeford, who immediately built a fine manor house on the estate. The Guldeford dynasty was to remain in occupation for over 300 years, during which time, in 1573, Elizabeth I and her entourage stayed there for three days.

In 1718, Sir Thomas Guldeford, with mounting debts and no heirs, sold Hempsted Park to Sir John Norris, who was Admiral of the British Fleet. In

Hempsted Park Terrace. (Painting by Jean Carpanini)

Benenden School's main entrance. (Painting by Jean Carpanini)

1857, a later owner, Gathorne Hardy, who became Earl of Cranbrook, demolished the Elizabethan house and built a new mansion to the designs of David Brandon. Finally, Harold Harmsworth, later Lord Rothermere (the founder of the *Daily Mail* and *Daily Mirror*), purchased the estate in 1910. He remodelled the house, divided up the estate and sold the house and immediate grounds of 250 acres to Benenden School in 1924.

The estate on which Benenden School resides is of great historical interest, but it is the general landscape in the heart of the Weald of Kent that is of special interest. The Weald of Kent was, until the late middle ages, the most densely forested region of England. The mighty oaks of the Weald were gradually thinned out when farmers from the Kentish uplands created clearings to feed their beasts on the abundant supply of acorns. These clearings were known as 'dens', hence the name Benenden. There are over thirty-four place names in Kent ending in the suffix 'den'. Timber for shipbuilding particularly during the Tudor period also denuded the oak forests.

Another contributory factor causing the mighty oaks of the Weald to be cleared was the emergence of the native English iron-smelting industry, fuelled by charcoal from the abundant oak trees and exploiting local iron ore deposits. The iron industry in Kent reached its peak in the late sixteenth century. In the seventeenth century, the industry moved to the coal-producing areas of south Wales and the north of England.

The setting of Benenden School in the Weald of Kent and the history of Hempsted Park have no doubt made more than just a passing impact on its pupils. Distinguished alumni include Anne, the Princess Royal; the journalist Penny Junor; actress Rachel Weisz; Sue Ryder and Eliza Manningham-Buller, a former Director General of MI5.

5

Cardinal Kempe's Wye Legacy, 1431

It is difficult to think of a 'Man of Kent' or indeed a 'Kentish Man' who achieved more in a lifetime than Cardinal John Kempe (1380–1454). His achievements in the service of his country were prodigious. He was a thoroughly political ecclesiastic whose clerical appointments were, as was the case in medieval England, a necessary concomitant to high political office. He held successively the bishoprics of Rochester (1419), Chichester (1421) and London (1421), becoming Archbishop of York in 1426 and Archbishop of Canterbury in 1452. During this period – in 1439 – Pope Eugenius IV offered Kempe the cardinal's hat.

John Kempe's political career proceeded in parallel with his ecclesiastical preferments, propelling him to comparable heights of achievement. He was in Normandy with Henry V at the time of Agincourt and became Chancellor of Normandy in 1419. When Henry V died from dysentery in 1422, Kempe returned to England to become part of the governing council assisting the infant Henry VI. He was twice Chancellor of England from 1426 to 1432 and again from 1450 until his death in 1454.

In the late-medieval period, the Chancellor's office was roughly equivalent to that of the Prime Minister today. Importantly, during his second period as Chancellor in 1450, by skilful and cunning negotiations, he saved Henry VI's crown by putting down Jack Cade's Kentish Rebellion after King Henry had fled from London to Kenilworth to escape from the advancing rebels. However, it is sad to record that Shakespeare gave him no credit for his achievements in his play *Henry VI, Part 2,* which dealt with Jack Cade's Rebellion.

Nevertheless, Kempe's enduring legacy will always be manifest in his native Wye, where he remodelled the parish church in cathedral-like style and size and founded a college alongside it, which was, until 2009, a world-famous agricultural centre for learning and research.

John Kempe was born in 1380 at 'Olantigh' in the parish of Wye, 2½ miles to the north of Ashford, on the banks of the River Stour. He was the second son of a Kentish gentleman, Thomas Kempe, and his wife, Beatrix, daughter of Sir Thomas Lewknor of Bodiam Castle in Sussex. They were, in the words of Edward Hasted, the eighteenth-century Kentish historian, 'a knightly family [viscounts] whose eldest sons were continuously granted Knighthoods until Sir Thomas Kempe's death in 1607'. He died without issue and 'Olantigh' passed into other hands after being in the family since the reign of Edward I in the thirteenth century.

The young John Kempe was baptised at the parish church of St Gregory in Wye and spent an idyllic childhood at 'Olantigh'. He received his childhood

'Olantigh', the Kempe family home for 400 years.

education at the Archbishop's School in Canterbury (now King's School) before attending Merton College Oxford, where he took a degree in law and became a fellow. He practised as a lawyer in the ecclesiastical courts and his undoubted talents were quickly spotted by the Archbishop of Canterbury, Thomas Arundel, who was also Lord Chancellor. Preferments both ecclesiastical and political quickly followed and thus began his meteoric rise in parallel careers.

His diplomatic peregrinations took him to Scotland, France and all over England in the service of both Henry V and his son, Henry VI. He was even instrumental in arranging the marriage of Henry VI to Margaret of Anjou and officiated at their wedding.

However, he always returned to his beloved 'Olantigh' to 'recharge his batteries' and, to this end, he built a chapel, or oratory, within its grounds. It was during these visits home that he hatched his plans to found a college in Wye whose purpose was to reinvigorate the worship of God in Wye's church – St Gregory, which was a central part of the college – and to educate the youth of the parish.

St Gregory's Church to which Wye College was dedicated.

In 1431, while in his first period as Chancellor, he obtained from the young Henry VI a licence to establish a college for secular priests in Wye, but to bring his plans to fruition he needed land on which to build it. The Royal Manor of Wye was owned by Battle Abbey and, no doubt after promising to rebuild St Gregory's Church, Kempe secured land adjoining the church that was sufficient to build his college. He also acquired from Battle Abbey the advowson (financial benefits) of the vicarage of Wye church and the surrounding farmlands. In addition, he settled a great deal of other property on his college to ensure its maintenance. This property was situated all over Kent and included church livings in Boughton Aluph, Brenzett and Newington. In Westwell, the estates of Perriton and Shottenden were settled, as was Perry Court near Wye, the Manor of Denne at Smarden and 'Old Surrenden'. These acquisitions were no doubt facilitated by the fact that he was not only Archbishop of York but also Chancellor of England.

Kempe's new foundation was called the College of St Gregory and St Martin, and its governing statutes were personally drawn up by Kempe with great assiduity, covering such matters as fines for fellows who did not attend the daily services and moderate punishments for choristers who

The front of Wye College. (Painting by Dennis Flanders)

played truant. Dice and games of chance were forbidden, as were women of doubtful character.

The head of the college was the master, or provost, and preference was to be given to graduates of his alma mater, Merton College Oxford. The rest of the establishment consisted of a grammar master, six secular priests (the fellows), two clerks, chaplains, two boy choristers and the scholars. Interestingly, under Kempe's statutes the grammar master was allowed to take private pupils outside school hours.

As soon as he obtained the advowson of St Gregory's he virtually rebuilt the church, enlarging it greatly to include three aisles and three chancels. He also remodelled the nave to give more light and the resultant cruciform church was magnificent, more like a minster in size and character. Kempe's college buildings were constructed immediately beyond the eastern boundary of the churchyard and matched perfectly the architecture of his new church. They consisted of a cloistered quadrangle enclosed by buildings of stone, flint and timber. The cloister pillars were originally oak. The buildings on the south side accommodated the master's residence and kitchens and were connected to the single-storey Latin school by a garden, which is now a superb specimen garden. The buildings on the north side of the quadrangle contained the Chapter House, lodgings and common room (today it also contains a small chapel). On the eastern side was the refectory (dining hall), known today as 'Old Hall', with its minstrels' gallery and the largest open crown roof in Kent. The western side of the quad was a plain screen wall with a gate leading to the church. The college eventually opened in 1447.

The old college buildings are still extant, although much has been added to the east of the original college, including the present-day entrance and Porter's Lodge and additional quadrangles. It is very Oxbridge in style and prior to its closure in 2009 it was part of Imperial College London. However, the same cannot be said of Kempe's Church of St Gregory and St Martin, for in 1686 the steeple and tower collapsed, demolishing the crossing, transepts and chancels. In the late eighteenth century, as if to ensure no further danger of collapse, the good people of Wye built a massive squat tower which totally overshadowed their new single chancel. Also, unusually, the tower is situated at the east end of the noticeably smaller church. In fact, the foundations of Kempe's original chancel are still visible today, extending 70ft or more to the east of the tower into the churchyard.

A modern addition that greatly enhances the church and includes a depiction of Cardinal Kempe is the beautiful stained glass Great West Window designed by Gerald Smith in 1951. It replaced an earlier window destroyed by enemy bombing in 1943.

Three years after Kempe opened his college, at the age of 70, he once again became Chancellor of England and two years later, in 1452, he was appointed Archbishop of Canterbury. He died in 1454 while holding the two most important posts in medieval England. Of Kempe's home, 'Olantigh', the grounds and estate remain intact in their idyllic riverside location on the south side of the Stour. Sadly, nothing remains of the medieval buildings, the mansion having been rebuilt thrice since Kempe's time. However, it is still privately owned and beautifully maintained.

Even though chroniclers throughout history have overlooked Kempe's extraordinary accomplishments, the architectural manifestations of his legacy cannot be ignored, and today they dominate Wye in the shape of the impressive church and the beautiful Wye College, whose future use has still not been finally decided, although Cardinal Kempe's original Latin school building has been taken over by the former students' Agricola Club as an exhibition centre.

The Latin School, Wye College's oldest building.

6

Jack Cade, Captain of Kent, 1450

Jack Cade is one of the greatest enigmas in English history. He claimed to be John Mortimer, a cousin of Richard, Duke of York, but in the 1450 rebellion which bears his name he was styled 'Captain of Kent'. He was thought to be Irish, possibly an illegitimate son of Edmund Mortimer, Earl of March, whose sister had married Richard, Duke of York. The Mortimers had considerable land holdings in Ireland. He was also said to have married a squire's daughter from Tandridge in Surrey. None of this can be proved. His true identity and status will probably never be known.

In the spring of 1450, he appears as from nowhere in Ashford in the county of Kent. It is here he first hears the 'Kentish Complaint', which was not confined to Kent but was a cogent example of a national malaise being experienced under Henry VI's incompetent and corrupt administration. The Hundred Years War with France had just concluded with the fall of Normandy, and England thereby lost all its French possessions with the exception of Calais. To prosecute this war, taxes had become punitive and the collectors of these on behalf of the king, the county sheriffs, had become extortioners. Henry VI had gathered around him a clique of second-ranking upstart nobles whose principal aim was personal enrichment, while serving a weak and erratic monarch.

The Duke of Suffolk, William de la Pole, despite a disastrous military record in France, became Chancellor in 1445. He was the king's prime minister and succeeded in marginalising the higher born and, in this instance, abler peers of the realm who were of Henry's blood. The Dukes of York, Exeter and

Gloucester all had potential claims to the throne, so naturally a weak king acquiesced to Suffolk's grand design.

It was in such a climate that James Fiennes, Lord Say and Sele of Knole Park, Sevenoaks, became Treasurer of England. He had, in a very short time, accumulated a spectacular list of lucrative honours and appointments: Lord Lieutenant of Kent, Warden of the Cinque Ports and Constable of Dover Castle. He, in turn, as is the way with nepotism, appointed his son-in-law, William Crowmer of Tunstall, near Sittingbourne, to the lucrative post of Sheriff of Kent.

In 1444, the Duke of Suffolk was instrumental in arranging Henry VI's marriage with a penniless French princess, Margaret of Anjou, and in return he ceded the territories of Anjou and Maine to her father. This was not well received by the already overtaxed English populace, who saw it as bad business, particularly as state finances were showing a record deficit.

The seeds being sown here are not those of Wat Tyler's Peasants' Revolt, seventy years earlier. On the contrary, the working people in the mid-fifteenth century had plentiful supplies of cheap food and wages were high. It was in the higher echelons of society where discontent was fermenting against government incompetence and oppressive taxes.

In January 1450, an exasperated Parliament, horrified by the loss of French possessions, impeached the Duke of Suffolk. However, the king intervened to mitigate the sentence to five years' exile in France as a guest of the Duke of Burgundy. The sense of national outrage at such a lenient sentence manifested itself in riots at Canterbury under Thomas Cheyne, a fuller (someone who beat, trod or bleached cloth to cleanse and thicken it), known as 'Blue Beard', who was executed for his pains.

However, full retribution was achieved on 2 May 1450, when the boat carrying Suffolk into exile was intercepted by the ship *Nicholas of the Tower*. He was summarily tried and executed, and his body was dumped on the beach at Dover by Kentish seamen. The king, and particularly Queen Margaret, were furious, and to assuage their anger, Lord Say and Sele, together with his son-in-law, Sheriff Crowmer, threatened to turn Kent into a deer park as punishment.

Thus, the stage was set. The deer park threat was the catalyst which drove the squires, gentlemen and yeoman of Kent into action. As has been said, there appeared in their midst one who claimed to be John Mortimer, a cousin of the Duke of York. He was distinguished in bearing, sophisticated and witty in speech and, above all, an experienced soldier. Although not yet 30 years of age, he was a veteran of campaigns in France and Ireland, having served with his kinsman, Richard, Duke of York.

Historians have always called him Jack Cade, as this was the name given in the warrant for his arrest made later. There can be no doubt that Jack Cade had the charisma, perspicacity and aristocratic bearing of a well-educated nobleman, so it was perfectly natural for the gentlemen of Kent to select him as their leader, the Captain of Kent.

At the end of May, the gentlemen of Kent decided to march to Blackheath to present their 'Bill of Complaints and Requests' to their king, not as adversaries but as loyal citizens anxious to protect the king from corrupt and unwise counsellors. They knew that contingents from Sussex and Surrey would be joining them. The uprising is given official status by the fact that constables of thirty-one Kent hundreds (out of a total of sixty-eight) called up fencible men in their area (a sort of Home Guard) to join the mass petition. Among the contingent were one knight, eighteen squires and seventy-four gentlemen. The distinguished families represented included those of seven past and future sheriffs. Their names are like a fifteenth-century *Who's Who* of Kent, including: Ballard, Bettenham, Cheyne, Clifford, Clifton, Culpepper, Fogge, Fyneux, Gulford, Lovelace, Norton and Tysden.

Among Cade's most trusted staff were Robert Poynings, his carver and sword-bearer, a disenchanted half-brother of Sheriff Crowmer, and Henry Wilkhous, his clerk, who was a notary and procurator to the Bishop of Rochester. After starting out from Ashford, Cade's army was joined at various points along the route by men from all over Kent but principally from Canterbury, Maidstone, Faversham and Dartford. By the time they reached Blackheath on 31 May, their numbers had swelled to around 20,000!

It is clear that many London merchants financed Cade – and for good reason. They were clearly unhappy with the incompetent government which had seen their trade greatly diminish. Also, they wanted to 'hedge their bets' in case Cade was successful in what was thought to be a Yorkist plot. Thomas Cocke, a past warden of the Drapers' Company, was Cade's go-between. Needing more money, Cade imposed an immediate levy in kind on all foreigners in the City of London. During the first week of June, Cade drew up the 'Bill of Complaints and Requests'.

On 7 June, the king was at Leicester attending Parliament when he heard of the Kentish rising. He returned to London, where he arrived on 13 June, and established himself at Clerkenwell. On 16 June, the king sent a deputation to Blackheath which included Cardinal John Kempe (see Chapter 5), his new chancellor and Archbishop of York, who had some sympathy for the rebels. Other members of the deputation included John Stafford, Archbishop of Canterbury, and the Duke of Buckingham. They received the 'Bill of Complaints and Requests' and agreed to deliver it to the king and return with his answer by a specific time.

No answer came. The king, in a fit of hubris, was in no mood to even consider their Bill.

Cade's intelligence indicated that the king was about to move against them with a force of 20,000. Such a respectable assembly of Kentish gentlemen did not wish to face the king's banner in the field as this would amount to treason. Also, Cade realised that his largely amateur force would be no match for the king's highly trained professional army on the open plains of Blackheath.

Cade ordered a tactical withdrawal to the wooded valleys around Sevenoaks and waited. The king sent a small contingent under Sir Humphrey Stafford to pursue Cade, but they were routed, and Stafford, his brother and twenty-four others were killed.

When news of this reached London, the king's army seemed to be on the verge of mutiny as they had much sympathy with the Kentish complaints. They demanded the heads of Lord Say and Sele and his son-in-law, Crowmer.

To placate the soldiers and to protect the two accused, the king consigned Lord Say and Crowmer to the Tower. He then sent the Archbishop of Canterbury and the Duke of Buckingham to negotiate with Cade. They reported back to the effect that Cade was a steadfast and formidable leader who was not prepared to back down. At this point, the king decided to flee to Kenilworth, Warwickshire, on 20 June, leaving Queen Margaret at Greenwich.

Cade spent the rest of June touring Kent to bolster support and to put right some of the injustices perpetrated, including restoration of seized land and removal of corrupt justices. He returned to Blackheath on 29 June, where he was joined by strong contingents from Sussex and Surrey.

On 2 July, the City Council voted to admit Cade into London despite the lone opposition of one alderman, Robert Horne. Cade established his headquarters in the White Hart in Southwark, on the south side of the Thames. On the same day, a large contingent arrived from Essex and occupied Mile End, just outside Aldgate. Cade entered the city in triumph and sat himself on the famous ceremonial London Stone in what is now Cannon Street and declared, 'Now is Mortimer Lord of this City?'

'Now is Mortimer Lord of this City'. Mortimer/Cade sat himself on the famous ceremonial London Stone.

Lord Saye and Sele being sentenced to death by Jack Cade.

On Saturday, 3 July, Cade again entered the city over London Bridge and immediately had Lord Say and Sheriff Crowmer indicted for treason by the Commission of Oyer and Terminer for London. The Lord Mayor of London, Sir Thomas Charlton, was a member of this commission. Lord Say was arraigned at the Guildhall and summarily executed by Cade's men in Cheapside. Crowmer was executed at Mile End by the Essex men. The heads of the two men were carried on poles throughout the city and made to kiss in a ghastly embrace and then placed on London Bridge.

Cade's need for money to provision his 20,000 men was, to some extent, his undoing. The good citizens of London did not mind him fining Alderman Horne 500 marks – he probably deserved it! And there was not too much protest when he ransacked the home of the deeply unpopular Alderman Malpass or seized jewels that were the property of the Duke of York (these were eventually returned to their owner on Cade's demise). However, after dining with citizen Curtis at his home in Tower Street, Cade insisted that his host contribute to his war chest. The city was outraged. What – or who – would be next?

The next day, Sunday, while Cade rested at the White Hart in Southwark, the Governor of the Tower, Lord Scales, a royalist, was persuaded by the city fathers that the men from Kent should be removed. He had under his command Matthew Gough, an experienced and brave soldier and veteran of the

Rochester Castle, where Cade sought refuge.

French War. It was he who led an attack on the rebel positions on London Bridge. The ensuing battle raged all night and there were many dead, including Gough. The outcome was undecided, and Cade was persuaded to enter negotiations.

The following morning, Monday, 6 July, the Archbishops of Canterbury and York, together with Bishop Wayneflete of Winchester, met Cade at St Margaret's Church, Southwark. They agreed, at last, formally to accept the Kentish 'Complaints and Requests' and to grant pardons to all those who had taken part in the rebellion, providing they withdrew and went home peaceably.

There were altogether 3,000 pardons issued on 6 and 7 July, under the authority of Queen Margaret, who was still at Greenwich. Cade, unlike most of his followers, was unhappy that the pardons could not at once be ratified by Parliament. However, on 8 July, he withdrew and made his way to Rochester Castle via Dartford. He had already arranged for the money and other spoils of war including the Duke of York's jewels to be transported by barge to Rochester. The Keeper of the Castle was a willing host while Cade and the rump of his army waited ostensibly for parliamentary ratification of their pardons.

Ripley Court, Hothfield, home of Alexander Iden, who captured Cade nearby.

However, on 10 July, the Exchequer issued a 'Writ and Proclamation by the King for the taking of Cade'. It offered 1,000 marks reward for bringing him, 'quick or dead', to the king and his council.

This is the first time he is referred to as Cade – until then he had been called John Mortimer. The writ goes on to allege that, a year before, Cade had dwelt in Sussex (Hurstpierpoint) in the employment of a knight called Sir Thomas Dacre, and while there, 'did murder a pregnant woman'. He is then alleged to have fled to France where he fought on the side of the French against the English! A very neat piece of character assassination bearing all the hallmarks of the wily old prelates, Kempe, Stafford and Wayneflete! In one fell swoop, they had technically removed the pardon issued to John Mortimer and attempted to blacken his character in the most heinous way. Conveniently, it seems there actually was a John Cade, Yeoman of Hurstpierpoint, who did abjure the realm in 1449.

Meanwhile, Cade, having stayed at Rochester for two days, inexplicably attacked Queenborough Castle, whose Keeper, Sir Roger Chamberlain, had been a trusted supporter. The attack failed and two of Cade's loyal lieutenants, Geoffrey Kechyn and Captain Boucher, were captured.

Cade was now on the run, and the same day his secretary, Henry Wilkhous, was arrested by Alexander Iden at Little Chart, near Hothfield, just outside Ashford. Alexander Iden lived nearby at Ripley Court (now Ripple Court), Hothfield, and was already in the pay of the Exchequer as Joint Protector of the Sea around Kent. However, it is doubtful whether he had at this time been appointed Sheriff of Kent. He was probably a bounty hunter who wished to impress the woman he loved, Elizabeth Crowmer, widow of the recently deceased Sheriff of Kent and daughter of the detested Lord Say and Sele.

A posse under Iden's command caught Cade on 13 July and mortally wounded him at Hothfield, in Kent, or Heathfield in Sussex – the jury is still out on this hotly debated issue. The only extant evidence is an entry in the Issue Rolls dated 21 October 1450 in which £20 is recorded as being paid to one John Davy for helping capture 'that great traitor John Mortimer at Hethfield, in the county of Sussex'. However, most contemporary accounts – and certainly Shakespeare – maintained that Hothfield was the place of Cade's arrest, although probably not in Alexander Iden's garden but a field nearby. Also, the arrest of Cade's secretary, Henry Wilkhous, at Little Chart would seem to support a Kent scene for Cade's final skirmish. Francis Newbury, who

Cades Road, Hothfield.

purchased Heathfield Park, Sussex, in 1784, seems to have hijacked the Cade legend by erecting a monument on the alleged scene of the crime at nearby Catte Street, which he renamed Cade Street.

After Cade's capture, Alexander Iden was appointed Sheriff of Kent and received his 1,000 marks reward. Additionally, he was appointed Governor of Rochester Castle and married the girl of his dreams, Elizabeth Crowmer. He moved to Tunstall, where the Crowmer family held the manor, but did not enjoy his good fortune for long. He died in 1457.

Cade's body was taken to London, where it was hung, drawn and quartered. His head adorned London Bridge as a warning to other potential rebels and the four parts of his body were separately despatched to four places where unrest had been manifest – Blackheath, Norwich, Salisbury and Gloucester.

However, the Kentish 'Complaint' was eventually considered because on 10 August 1450, a special Commission of Oyer and Terminer, headed by the two Archbishops, Kempe and Stafford, was sent into Kent to enquire into the grievances. Eight men were hanged at Canterbury for remaining in arms after receiving pardons.

The Duke of York arrived back from Ireland at the end of August and in December was given a poisoned chalice by the king. Sporadic rioting was still taking place in Kent, so the king appointed the Duke of York to head a commission to visit Kent and deal with the rebels. Forty-one executions took place, becoming known in Kent as the 'Harvest of Heads'. It is doubtful whether the Duke of York in fact visited Kent, but the commission bore his name and made him deeply unpopular in the county; so much so that in the Wars of the Roses, which immediately followed, Kent did not rise in support of the Yorkist cause.

Issues surrounding Cade's rebellion, such as his antecedence, his place of capture and the possibility of a Yorkist plot, will always be hotly debated. However, it is indisputable that he did have London and the kingdom within his grasp. Why did he hesitate at various key moments? Perhaps he was in danger of exceeding his brief and his Svengali – the Duke of York? – was not quite ready to take centre stage. What a waste of a truly great and good rebel.

Oliver Cromwell, 200 years later, did not make the same mistake.

7

The Tokes of Godinton, 1496

The Toke family resided at Godinton Park in the parish of Great Chart, a mile to the east of Ashford, for more than 400 years (*c.*1490–1896). Unlike their politically motivated neighbours, the Tuftons of Hothfield, the Derings of Pluckley and the Darrels of Calehill (Little Chart), they were content most of the time to be gentlemen farmers and local squires. They were not acquisitive in terms of land ownership as a source of income and they were satisfied with working their surrounding lands and renting any extra land needed for farming purposes.

Godinton as it is today.

In the mid-seventeenth century, the Tuftons (by then Earls of Thanet) were the wealthiest family in Kent at £10,000 a year, while the Derings and Darrels supplemented rental earnings with income from government appointments, probably amounting to about £2,000 a year. Receiving their income purely from farming, the Tokes probably never achieved more than £400 a year at this time (although this was still a considerable sum). However, their great achievement and lasting legacy, unlike their more illustrious neighbours, was to keep a large part of the estate (950 acres) intact. Today, the only visible evidence of the Tuftons, Derings and Darrels is confined to a beleaguered stable block or the odd garden wall and the ubiquitous Dering windows adorning cottages around Pluckley. In contrast, the Tokes' Godinton estate, bounded to the south by the River Stour, is one of Kent's finest visitor attractions, with buildings and formal gardens on a par with Sissinghurst and Penshurst Place.

The first recorded owners of Godinton were a family of that name, it being a custom of Norman families to take the name of the property they owned. The first mention I have found is in *Archaeological Cantiana, Vol. VI*, which alludes to an old document dated 1197 and recording the death of a Simon de Godinton, who was succeeded by his son, Stephen.

At this time, the Godintons also owned manors in Strood and Chelsfield, which were sold in 1327 by William Godinton. His son Alan is recorded in documents of the period as being Lord of Godinton Manor in 1347.

It is thought that the original Godinton House was built in 1165, presumably during Simon Godinton's time. In the late fourteenth century, the house was sold to the Champney family who, after a short period, sold it to Thomas Goldwell, from the nearby manor of Goldwell, then the principal manor in the area. The Goldwells had been resident at Goldwell Manor since around 1200 and were to continue in ownership there until the early seventeenth century when the manor was acquired by Sir John Tufton, newly arrived at Hothfield, as part of his family's acquisition plans.

The Toke coat of arms.

Thomas was John Goldwell's youngest son and took up residence at the relatively humble Godinton residence in 1405. In turn, he was succeeded by his son, William, on whose death in 1485 the estate passed into the hands of the

The Great Hall.

Captain Nicholas Toke.

Toke family through the marriage of his daughter Joan to Thomas Toke, Lord of the Manor of Bere, near Dover. Although they were both dead before 1485, their youngest son John inherited Godinton at some point after this date.

John Toke Senior served Henry VII with great distinction, acting in 1495 as an emissary with the French court against the imposter Perkin Warbeck. For this service, he was awarded an augmentation to the Toke coat of arms in the addition of three greyhounds. He died in 1513 and was succeeded by a son, John, who had married Cecily Kempe from 'Olantigh', Wye. Her Uncle Thomas was Bishop of London, and her great uncle was Cardinal John Kempe, whom we met in Chapter 5.

The present Godinton manor house is Jacobean in appearance, but it is built around the core of the late-fourteenth-century Great Hall, with its magnificent chestnut tie beam and crown post. The Godwells would no doubt have created what would have been a typical Kentish hall house which the Tokes did not change much during their early occupation.

Then along came the most illustrious of the Toke dynasty, Captain Nicholas Toke, who owned and ran the estate for more than fifty years. Facts about his early life are sketchy: he almost certainly gained his military rank from the Royalist army, but it is believed that he also had a naval career between 1621 and 1624 and served in the West Indies.

Before his father, John, died in 1627, Captain Toke had married four times. His second wife, Margaret (daughter of Thomas Knatchbull, heir apparent to Mersham le Hatch, whose wife was a niece of the Duke of Suffolk), was the most aristocratic of any previous Mrs Toke. This marriage in 1616 coincided with Nicholas leasing the Godinton farms from his father. With such a high-born wife, a more fitting house was needed, and thus began the rebuilding and enlargement of Godinton. However, Margaret died in 1618, leaving two daughters.

Two years later, Captain Toke tried marriage again, to Mrs Barham, a widow, who sadly died after only a year. In 1622, he married again – Mary, daughter of Sir Anthony Browne of Wild Hall, Essex, who lived until 1640. It is her initials 'MT', along with 'NT', that appear on drawing room and library chimney pieces.

Captain Nicholas Toke rebuilt and extended the existing house in Jacobean style, adding the east wing and dining room. However, the *pièce de résistance* was the remarkable carved main staircase which he added to the northern flank of the medieval great hall, extending over the courtyard. It was carved in chestnut and is an eclectic mix of Jacobean and medieval motifs containing

Captain Toke's remarkable carved chestnut staircase.

many 'queer beasts' and, with together with that at Knole, is one of the most lavish staircases in England.

The most beautiful and original interior at Godinton is the great chamber on the first floor. What makes the room extraordinary are the friezes on the west and north walls representing various movements in musketry and pike drill. The focal point is undoubtedly Captain Toke's remarkable carved chimney-piece. The centre panel is occupied by the Toke arms, with the frieze above carved with figures illustrating pig sticking, bear baiting and hunting, his favourite pursuits. Interestingly, the chimney-piece was transposed to the adjacent parlour, or priest's room, when it was used as the setting for a painting called 'The Last Day in the Old Home' (1862) by the pre-Raphaelite painter R.B. Martineau. The painting, which also features the great staircase, transposed from the great hall, now hangs in the Tate Britain gallery.

Incidentally, at least two of the fireplaces at Godinton are undisputedly made of local Bethersden marble from the Daniels Water quarry, a mile away. These are situated in the great hall and dining room and clearly exhibit the characteristics of Bethersden marble – conglomerated fossil shells. Most famously, Bethersden marble can be found in Canterbury and Rochester cathedrals.

One of Captain Toke's lasting achievements are his detailed farm accounts, which he kept from 1616 to 1680. They represent a full and thorough account of farming life in the seventeenth century and were published as such by the British Academy in 1927.

However, success on the estate was not matched by a similar achievement in producing an heir. Despite his many marriages, Captain Toke only had daughters, but he did not give up, and in 1642 he married for a fifth time. However, Lady Diana Finch, daughter of the Earl of Winchelsea, from nearby Eastwell Manor, died in 1667 without producing a son. So, Captain Toke adopted his nephew, also called Nicholas, who duly inherited Godinton on his uncle's death in 1680. He remained remarkable even to the day he died, when, aged 92, he was travelling to London in pursuit of a sixth bride!

The younger Nicholas dutifully maintained the farm accounts until 1703 and, like his uncle before him in 1663, was Sheriff of Kent in 1693. A year later, he was knighted and became Sir Nicholas Toke.

The next five generations of Tokes continued in residence at Godinton, devoting their time mainly to farming their lands and being worthy citizens of Kent. One of their number became MP for East Grinstead, while another, John, became another Toke Sheriff of Kent in 1770.

Probably the most influential of the eighteenth- and nineteenth-century Tokes was Nicholas Roundell Toke (1764–1837). His mother, Margaret Eleanor Roundell, was an heiress and he also married an heiress, Anne Maria Wrey, so consequently, he had considerably more money to spend than most of his ancestors. He furnished Godinton in great style, with rich carvings and wonderful medieval stained glass.

He was aided in this glorifying process by Thomas Willement of Davington Priory, near Faversham, a celebrated designer and antiquarian and an important figure in the Renaissance movement in the early nineteenth century. It was under his influence that most of the stained glass still beautifying Godinton today was acquired.

Sadly, Nicholas Roundell Toke's grandson, Colonel John Toke, became the black sheep of the family by selling Godinton. He was a professional soldier, who had no interest in farming or estate management and had even moved out to Camberley in Surrey. This move was no doubt aided by a scandalous divorce case at the time, caused by his affair with a neighbour's wife. The situation was exacerbated by the agricultural depression of the late nineteenth century, with family debts adding to the financial strain. After a succession of tenants, Godinton was sold in 1895 to George Ashley Dodd, thereby ending 400 years of continuous Toke family occupation.

The family church for both the Goldwells and the Tokes was St Mary's, Great Chart, a mile south of Godinton, and the north chapel is their mausoleum. In addition, there are many memorials to both families, particularly the Tokes, and headstones in the graveyard.

George Ashly Dodd employed the eminent Victorian architect and garden designer, Sir Reginald Blomfield, to carry out extensive renovations and remodelling of the rooms at Godinton. He also designed the magnificent formal gardens which immediately surround the house, in contrast to the earlier open landscape style. To complete his formal design, he enclosed the gardens with a boundary yew hedge extending to more than 1,500ft, which is claimed to be the longest in England.

After Ashley Dodd's death in 1917, Godinton was sold to the Hon. Mrs Bruce Ward, daughter of the 1st Lord Dovedale, who, with her husband and family, lavished much love and attention on Godinton. She was a renowned hostess and socialite and amassed an extensive collection of fine antiques and paintings which, along with the Toke collection, can still be found on display today.

Mrs Bruce Ward died in 1952 and was succeeded by her maternal grandson, Major Alan Wyndham Green. He never married but continued the policy of maintenance and enhancement for forty-four years until his death in 1996. Four years before he died, he established the Godinton Charitable Trust, richly endowed from land sales, which ensured Godinton's future posterity for the benefit of the nation.

8

Father of the English Sonnet: Sir Thomas Wyatt, 1503

According to Kent historian Edward Hasted, Sir Thomas Wyatt (1503–42) was the indisputable father of the English sonnet, and Allington Castle, near Maidstone, was its cradle. Without him, there might not have been any Shakespearean sonnets, Hasted asserts.

Thomas Wyatt is credited with introducing the fourteen-line poem to England and wrote thirty himself. Although they would have been recited at Court, none were published during his lifetime and, consequently, like many creative geniuses, Wyatt's true worth was not appreciated until after his death. However, throughout his lifetime, he did achieve fame and distinction as an influential diplomat and courtier, who was much admired for his charismatic wit and charm as well as his poetry. He was a great favourite of both Henry VIII and Anne Boleyn, whose lover he was reputed to be.

Sir Thomas Wyatt.

Thomas Wyatt's ancestors were influential Yorkshiremen. His grandfather, Sir Richard Wyatt, born in 1428 at Mexborough, moved south and became

High Sheriff of London. Likewise, his father Henry, also born in Mexborough in 1460, made his fortune in London, mainly as reward for his support and loyalty to the aspiring Henry Tudor in his fight with Richard III. This was unusual – a Yorkshire man supporting a Lancastrian cause. And yet, after taking part in an unsuccessful revolt against Richard III, Henry Wyatt was imprisoned in Scotland for two years, refusing to renounce his loyalty to Henry Tudor, despite torture and starvation. He only survived, so the legend goes, because a prison cat brought him pigeons which a sympathetic guard cooked for him.

After the Battle of Bosworth in 1485, the newly crowned Henry VII rewarded Henry's loyalty by making him a privy councillor and executor of his will. Such was his position at Court that by 1492, Henry Wyatt was wealthy enough to purchase Allington Castle on the banks of the Medway, which he greatly restored to some splendour.

It was here that Thomas Wyatt was born in 1503, and from an early age he mixed in distinguished company when the likes of Henry VII, Cardinal Wolsey and Henry VIII would visit his father on diplomatic matters. In 1515, at the age of 12, Thomas entered St John's College Cambridge, which had been founded four years earlier by Henry VII's mother, Margaret Beaufort.

Allington Castle.

A year later, Henry introduced his son to life at Court. Thomas served as a Sewer Extraordinary (a servant who waited at the royal table) and then held a succession of domestic appointments including, in 1524, Clerk of the King's Jewels under his father's direction as Keeper.

In 1520, aged just 17, Thomas married Elizabeth Brooke, daughter of Lord Cobham, a close neighbour. Although two children quickly followed, the marriage only lasted four years before the couple separated on the grounds of Elizabeth's adultery. By this time, Thomas was engaging in courtly love with a succession of adoring ladies at Court, including the 17-year-old Anne Boleyn.

The Boleyns of Hever Castle were neighbours and associates of the Wyatts, and Anne, who had recently returned from finishing school in France, was making quite an impression at the English Court with her sophisticated French ways. Thomas was openly writing poetry describing life at Court, and Anne, in particular. The exact nature of their relationship isn't clear, but in his poetry, Thomas calls her his 'mistress Anna' and embeds events in her life into his verse.

However, as soon as Anne caught the eye of Henry VIII he determined to rid the Court of any of her suitors. In 1524, in the tilt yard at Greenwich, the Court staged the 'Castle of Loyalty', a mock battle whereby four 'maidens of the court', including Anne, were defended by fifteen courtiers, including Thomas. The attackers included Henry Percy, who had become secretly engaged to Anne Boleyn.

Into the fray stepped Henry VIII, who proceeded to thrash his opponents as if giving notice that Anne was his. Thomas's poem, '*Whoso List to Hunt*', is said to be an allegory referring to Anne's courtship by the king and Thomas's acknowledgement that Anne had become the property of the king alone.

Wyatt was subsequently assigned to foreign missions. His first ambassadorial appointment in 1526 took him to Cognac in France as assistant to his Kentish neighbour, Sir Thomas Cheney of Shurland Manor, on the Isle of Sheppey. The trip's purpose was to congratulate Francis I, on behalf of Henry VIII, on his safe delivery from captivity at the hands of Emperor Charles V of Spain (at the time, Spain was the most powerful nation in Europe). Thomas earned golden plaudits from all concerned for his charm and diplomacy, all of which were communicated to Cardinal Wolsey and Henry VIII.

The following year, he accompanied Sir John Russell to Italy to offer English support to the Pope against the Spanish invaders. While on a fruitless exercise to Venice, Thomas was captured by the invaders, but managed to escape and make his way back to Rome from where he and Sir John departed just before it was sacked by the Spanish.

Thomas's time in Italy was of incredible significance and influenced his development as a poet. He was greatly impressed with Italian literature, particularly the poems of Petrarch and Plutarch, which he enthusiastically interpreted and disseminated on his return to England. In fact, Queen Catherine of Aragon was greatly impressed and Wyatt translated Plutarch's 'Quyete and Mynde' for her, a deeply philosophical treatise on humanism. As a result, Thomas and Queen Catherine developed a great intellectual respect for one another.

In 1528, Thomas was made High Marshall of Calais, a post he held for four years, which culminated in hosting Henry VIII and his acknowledged mistress, Anne Boleyn, on a visit to Calais just a few months before they married. Thomas was then called back to England to carry out several domestic missions on behalf of Thomas Cromwell who, by this time, had succeeded Wolsey as the definite power behind the throne.

Wyatt's rehabilitation was complete when he served as Chief Ewer at Anne's coronation in 1533 and his diplomatic career began to blossom, with new appointments coming thick and fast. He was appointed a Justice of the Peace for Essex, High Steward of the Abbey at West Malling, Commander-in-Chief for Kent in case of war, and finally, was knighted on Easter Day, 1535.

Meanwhile, he continued to write. His poetry had always reflected the inherent dangers and reversals of fortune at the Tudor Court, none more so than in 1536 when Anne Boleyn was accused by Henry VIII of adultery and despatched to the Tower along with six alleged lovers, including Thomas Wyatt himself.

It is thought that Wyatt wrote 'V Innocentia Veritas Viat Fides Circumdederunt me inimici mei' after witnessing her execution from his cell in the Bell Tower, with his sorrow evident in the lines:

These bloody days have broken my heart.
        My lust, my youth did then depart,
And blind desire of estate.
        Who hastes to climb seeks to revert.
Of truth, circa Regna tonat.

The Bell Tower showed me such sight
        That in my head sticks day and night.

There did I learn out of a grate,
For all favour, glory, or might,
That yet circa Regna tonat.

Thomas probably escaped death because his alleged affair with Anne took place before she became queen. His only punishment was to be sent home to Allington to learn, under his father's supervision, 'to conduct himself in a more seemly fashion'.

However, his fall from grace was short-lived because in the autumn of 1536, in his role as Commander-in-Chief for Kent, he helped Henry VIII defeat an uprising in the north of England. Protesting against Henry VIII's religious policies, the Pilgrimage of Grace was triggered by the dissolution of the monasteries and rumours of the closure of churches, although there were also underlying economic and social reasons for the dissent.

Shortly afterwards, Thomas was appointed Sheriff of Kent and then, in November, his father died, and he became master of Allington. At around the same time, his son Thomas, aged 15, was married to Jane Hawte of Bishopsbourne, co-heiress of Sir William Hawte. During the reign of Mary I, Thomas the Younger led a rebellion against that Catholic monarch, which resulted in his execution.

Thomas Senior lived openly with his long-term mistress, Elizabeth Darrell, having first returned his adulterous wife to her family at Cobham. Elizabeth had been a trusted lady-in-waiting to Catherine of Aragon and a minor beneficiary in her will.

In March 1537, Thomas was appointed Ambassador to the Imperial Court in Spain. England's standing in Europe was at a very low point. The schism with Rome and a Catholic alliance between Italy, France and Spain was a great threat to English security. It was thought that Thomas's diplomatic skills could somehow help destabilise the Catholic alliance by getting Emperor Charles I of Spain to support England's position.

It was a hopeless venture, particularly in view of what had happened to Charles's cousin, Catherine of Aragon, who King Henry wished to divorce. Nevertheless, Charles and Thomas developed an excellent rapport and no harm was done. He finally returned to England in 1540 and his great mentor Thomas Cromwell made sure that his efforts on behalf of his country did not go unrewarded. He received the property of two monasteries that Cromwell had suppressed – Boxley Abbey near Allington and the Priory of Crutched Friars in London.

However, later that year, Cromwell was arrested for diverse treasonable offences, including the fiasco that was Henry VIII's marriage to Anne of Cleves, very much a Cromwell project. Within months, Henry had married Catherine Howard, and Cromwell was executed during the nuptials.

Wyatt turned to the pen once more, prophetically writing 'The lover laments the death of his love' to commemorate the death of his old mentor, Thomas Cromwell.

With Cromwell out of the way, Wyatt was unprotected from his former enemies and old charges of treason were revisited. He was seized, bound and consigned to the Tower. This further reversal of Tudor fortunes is alluded to in his most famous poem, which begins:

They flee from me that sometime did me seek,
With naked foot stalking in my chamber.
I have seen them gentle tame and meek
That now are wild and do not remember
That sometime they put themselves in danger
To take bread at my hand; and now they range
Busily seeking with a continual change.

Thanked be fortune, it hath been otherwise
Twenty times better; but once in special,
In thin array after a pleasant guise,
When her loose gown from her shoulders did fall,
And she me caught in her arms long and small;
And Therewithall sweetly did me kiss,
And softly said, 'Dear heart, how like you this?'

It was no dream, I lay broad waking.
But all is turned thorough my gentleness
Into a strange fashion of forsaking;
And I have leave to go of her goodness
And she also to use newfangleness.
But since that I so kindly am served,
I would fain know what she hath deserved.

In true Wyatt style, he launched into a spirited defence of his actions and wrote impassioned letters to Henry VIII. Assisted by the powerful Howard family, including Queen Catherine, a relieved Henry joyfully released his old friend.

The remaining year of his life was filled with vigorous endeavour and achievement. He was sent by Henry to defend Calais in the early part of 1542, was elected MP for Kent a few months later and, in October, was sent in great haste to Falmouth to meet the newly arrived Spanish Ambassador. However, on this final journey he caught a fever and died on 11 October 1542.

In an adventurous life, it is true to say that Sir Thomas Wyatt was the all-round Renaissance man – governor, soldier, diplomat, linguist and distinguished man of letters.

9

Princess Pocahontas: A Gravesend Enigma, 1617

On 21 March 2017, a gathering took place at St George's Church, Gravesend, to celebrate the life of an American citizen who died in Gravesend exactly 400 years to the day before this memorable event. Her name was Rebecca Rolfe, and she was a Native American. The celebrants included the American Ambassador Matthew Barzum, the Mayor of Gravesham, Greta Goatley, the Reverend Canon Chris Stone, Rector of St George's Church, and John Rolfe, a direct descendant of Rebecca Rolfe. It was the beginning of a week-long programme of events to celebrate the life of a woman who died tragically at the age of 20 at Gravesend while travelling back to Virginia after having been a guest of King James I.

A contemporary painting of Pocahontas a few months before her death.

But why all the fuss about a young girl of 20 by the prosaic name of Rolfe? Mrs Rolfe was Native American royalty; she was none other than Princess Pocahontas, the daughter of Powhatan, the most powerful Algonquin First Nation

Chief in seventeenth-century America. She is a historical icon, without whom there may not have arisen the United States of America. She is truly the mother of the nation, whose ancestors formed the backbone of the fledgling British colony that was early America.

A romanticised Disney cartoon film was made in 1995 called *Pocahontas*, which, in true Hollywood style, had but a passing resemblance to the true history of one of the most momentous events in world history.

Pocahontas was born in about 1595, the daughter of Chief Powhatan, who ruled over the villages along the rivers, now named James and York, that flowed into Chesapeake Bay in what is now Virginia. Her name means 'playful little girl' and it was changed by her father from her birth name Matoaka.

She would play a vital role in the establishment of the first successful permanent British settlement in America in 1588. But why was the area around Chesapeake Bay chosen, and who made that choice? Sir Walter Raleigh, who had financed several attempts to settle in America – principally at Roanoke Island – since 1585, was keen to stay well clear of the Spanish settlement in Florida. With the promise of untold supplies of gold and silver in this area, a healthy distance north of Florida, Queen Elizabeth in 1584 granted Raleigh Letters Patent to found a settlement in the area, which Raleigh named Virginia after the Virgin Queen. But she made the granting of such a licence conditional on Raleigh himself not risking his life in being part of the exploration team. He was too valuable to her.

All his attempts ended in failure, principally because the early settlers could not cope with the harsh conditions encountered. They were unable to feed themselves and faced hostility from the local First Nation tribes. The failure came at great personal cost to Raleigh of around £40,000.

The ascension of James I to the throne on Elizabeth's death in 1603 resulted in two events which changed the nature of further expeditions to Virginia. First, Raleigh was arrested and eventually executed for high treason for allegedly plotting James I's downfall. Then there was a decision to set up the Virginia Trading Company on similar lines to the immensely successful East India Company.

The first expedition under the auspices of the Virginia Company set sail from Blackwall, Greenwich, in three small ships, *Godspeed*, *Discovery* and *Susan Constant,* under the command of Captain Newport. Their destination was Chesapeake Bay in Virginia, where they were, according to precise instructions from the Virginia Company, to set up a settlement that was strategically well positioned defensively on a three-sided peninsula at the mouth of two rivers and in a deep-water harbour. This was far enough inland to be inconspicuous to the Spanish ships passing to and from their Florida settlement. A triangular fort was to be built for protection from the local Native Americans. In addition, each ship carried a sealed box which contained the names of the seven council leaders who were to govern the new colony.

The party of 105 included a preacher, doctor, carpenters and other craftsmen who would be useful in constructing the fort and other buildings. But the most important members of the expeditionary force were two experienced soldiers, Edward Maria Wingfield, of noble blood, and the relatively lowly born Captain John Smith, who at the young age of 27 had fought in campaigns in Holland, in mid-Europe for the Austrians against the Turks, and had been a pirate and a soldier of fortune: in short, a mercenary. He was from Norfolk, where his father had been estate manager to the noble Willoughby family and young John had been brought up alongside the Willoughby sons and had learnt the basic skills of military accomplishment, such as swordsmanship and rifle and pistol use.

It was inevitable that the haughty, noble-born Wingfield and Smith would clash. And this led to Smith being imprisoned for most of the voyage after Wingfield's accusation to Captain Newport that Smith planned to mutiny and proclaim himself as king of the new colony. As a result, he did not witness the first sight of Virginia when the ships arrived at their destination in late April 1607.

Initially, on landing, the pugnacious Captain Smith was still held as a prisoner and did not go on the first exploration upriver with Wingfield and a small party. However, when one of the sealed boxes was opened and Smith was named as one of the ruling council, he was released. As Captain Newport was soon to be returning to England, a vote of some kind was taken, and Maria Wingfield was chosen as the president of the new colony.

Smith set to work with the others to pitch tents, lay out garden plots and carry out the orders issued by Wingfield. Every day, he expected there would be some military drill inaugurated, but no, there was no mention of it. No fortification or protection was planned except for a pile of loose boughs heaped up in a half-circle. What possible use would they be in case of an attack?

If he had mentioned the word 'fort', however, he would doubtless have been laughed at and scorned. Where, pray, would you get stones in this stoneless land to construct a fort? John Smith could have told them, had they asked him, about forts he had seen in the backwoods of Poland and Hungary that were built entirely of logs ... About ten days later, the settlement was attacked by Native Americans and President Wingfield had an arrow shot through his beard – this considerably altered his viewpoint.

John Smith was not there at the time, nor was Captain Newport. They had gone with twenty others in small open boats to explore and discover, if they could, the source of the Chickahominy River, which emptied into the James. They found the Native Americans friendly, especially one named Navirans, who acted as a guide and drew a map of the rivers.

However, in some way, he aroused the suspicions of Captain Newport that all was not well and they hurried back to Jamestown. They found that the day before, while the men were at work, with their guns stored in fat to keep them from rusting, the settlement had been attacked by Native Americans. Seventeen men were hurt, one boy killed, and if a shot had not been fired from the ship's cannon, which scared off the attackers, there would have been an end to the plantation. President Wingfield, who had felt the arrow whizz through his beard, was now 'contented', as John Smith said, 'that a palisade of logs fort should be constructed'.

The following day, the Native Americans sent word that they desired peace, so Captain Newport felt able to return to England.

It was June, and 100 hundred settlers were left in Virginia. By mid-September, fifty of them were dead, and most of the others were so weak from malaria and typhoid fever that they could scarcely bury the dead. Only the president was well.

They were living on sturgeon and sea crabs, half a pint of wheat a day and half a pint of barley, boiled with water. The grain had been in the ship's hold and contained as many worms as kernels. Only President Wingfield was obviously well fed.

The dissatisfaction with Wingfield was so great that the members of the council deposed him and John Smith became the natural leader of the colony. He took six or seven men down the river with some beads and hatchets to trade and came back with food – oysters, venison, wild turkey and sixteen bushels of corn. He set to work with the men and got them to build houses and thatch them.

The Native Americans continued to supply the settlers with food throughout the summer and autumn. But by December, they grew tired of the constant demands being made of them by the settlers, sometimes with the threat of force. One of Powhatan's chiefs captured Captain Smith, who was then brought

Pocahontas saves Captain John Smith's life.

before Powhatan. It looked as though he was about to be executed with his head on a block when Pocahontas was said to have run from her father's side and placed her head over his, thus preventing the execution. There is a theory that it was all part of a ritual as a prelude to Smith being recognised as a friend and the 'Great Chief' of the settlers and to be received into the tribe.

Pocahontas became a regular visitor to the Jamestown colony, where in 1608, John Smith was duly elected President of the Jamestown Council. However, a year later, while he was resting, a spark from his pipe set light to his powder bag, which was on his lap. It caused terrible injuries to his upper thighs, which were to render him impotent. He was immediately shipped back to England on the next available ship.

In the meantime, John Rolfe arrived from Heacham, Norfolk, with his wife, who died shortly after arrival in Jamestown. Crucially for the colony, he brought tobacco seeds from Trinidad, which produced a leaf more palatable than the coarse local variety. Tobacco saved the colony and by 1618 it was exporting 50,000lb a year – a vast amount.

But before the economic benefits were fully realised, the colony desperately needed to secure its food supply and to maintain good relations with the Native Americans. In 1613, the colonists captured Pocahontas and held her as a hostage in Jamestown. She was actually treated as an honoured guest but the ruse succeeded in securing good relations between Powhatan and the English. During the next year, Pocahontas was in the care of the Calvinist minister Alexander Whitaker, instructed in the Christian faith and duly converted to Christianity.

John Rolfe fell in love with Pocahontas and asked permission to marry her from the Governor, Sir Thomas Dale. He duly agreed, seeing this as another knot to bind the peace with the local tribes, particularly as Powhatan also consented, sending two sons as witnesses and her uncle to give her away. She had been baptised Rebecca, and her marriage took place on 5 April 1614. Rolfe was appointed Secretary and Recorder of the Colony.

In April 1616, the Virginia Company arranged for the Rolfes to visit England on what was a gigantic PR exercise to raise awareness of the colony and promote further investment and immigration. When King James realised that Rebecca Rolfe was a Native American princess he was somewhat irked that his permission had not been sought by John Rolfe to marry foreign royalty and as a result, they became his honoured guests. The Rolfes also took with them their infant son, Thomas, and a dozen Native Americans, who attracted much curiosity. The Virginia colony was now well and truly on the map.

Having landed first at Plymouth, on 3 June 1616, they proceeded to London by ship. They stayed only a few days before beginning the journey to the Rolfe family home at Heacham in Norfolk. On the way, they met King James at Newmarket and watched the races with him, which Rebecca greatly enjoyed along with the king's company. They carried on to Heacham, where they stayed for the whole summer at the family home.

Rebecca really loved her time in Heacham and was sorry when they had to return to London with its noise and smells. She met Sir Walter Raleigh and had dinner with the Bishop of London. She attended the Christmas Masque with the king and queen and in February, a 'Masque of Lovers Made Men' was given for the French Ambassador, which was also attended by Rebecca, the king, queen and the Lord Mayor.

The London air did not agree with Pocahontas, and she became unwell. They sought better air at Brentford, where she met John Smith again at what proved to be a most uncomfortable encounter for both parties.

The Rolfes sailed for home in March 1617, but at Gravesend, where they stopped to take on fresh food and water, she was taken ill (probably tuberculosis) and she was brought ashore either dead or dying. She was buried in the chancel of the Parish Church of St George on 21 March 1617.

St George's Church, where Pocahontas was buried, with her statue in the foreground. (Painting by Janet Davie)

There is, however, one error in the burial register, which says, 'March 21 Rebecca Wrolfe wyfre of *Thomas* [author's emphasis] Wrolfe gent. A Virginian lady borne, was buried in ye Chancell.'

John Rolfe and young Thomas recommenced their journey, but at Plymouth, young Thomas was landed to await collection by John Rolfe's brother, Henry, who would fetch him back to London. It was thought that he would not survive the journey back to Virginia.

Thomas eventually returned to Virginia in 1635. His grandfather, Powhatan, had died in 1618, a year after his mother. He married Jane Poythress and their only child, Jane, married Colonel Robert Bolling in 1675. Their numerous descendants claim a bloodline to Pocahontas.

In 1896, a memorial tablet to Pocahontas was placed in the chancel of St George's Church and in 1914, memorial windows were presented by the Colonial Dames of America. In 1922, a bronze statue of Pocahontas by the sculptor William Partridge was unveiled in Jamestown, Virginia. Later, in 1958, a replica of the Jamestown Pocahontas statue was presented to the British people by the Governor of Virginia and resides at the entrance to St George's Church.

Although there are plenty of memorials to Pocahontas, there are precious few artefacts of a contemporary nature associated with her, except for a Simon van de Pass engraving made from a portrait created in England in the last few months of her life. No one knows what happened to the original portrait. Pocahontas is dressed in the English fashion in rich shades of red, gold and green, with lace cuffs and high collar. However, her skin, hair and eye colour have been significantly lightened. Copies of the engraving are held in the British Museum, the Royal Collection Trust and the National Portrait Gallery in Washington DC. Many people are greatly disappointed when they view this engraving as she looks not at all 'exotic'. Her sombre look could be attributed to the fact that she was probably showing symptoms of the illness from which she died a short while later.

All other portraits are either based on this engraving or are romanticised portrayals painted much later, including the Sedgeford Hall portrait of Pocahontas and her son, Thomas Rolfe, which now hangs in Kings Lynn Town Hall.

The skeleton of Pocahontas has never been found, despite a thorough archaeological excavation in 1923, which proved fruitless. All that was discovered were bones of a pig, a sheep, an ox, a dog, and a cat, and the remains of 130 individuals which had no resemblance to Pocahontas. The task was made more difficult by the fact that the original St George's Church was burnt down in 1727 and its replacement (the present-day church) was built in a slightly different location. There has always been a rather gruesome alternative explanation circulating, that the coffin of Pocahontas was stolen by body snatchers and taken up the river to London where their attempts to sell it were foiled. The body was reinterred and all traces of it were lost. Pending further discoveries or research, the exact whereabouts of Pocahontas's earthly remains will remain a secret she took to her grave.

Heacham Hall, the home of the Rolfe family was (like many stately homes) occupied by the armed forces during the Second World War and accidentally destroyed by fire in the 1940s.

The 1923 archaeological examination of tombs in St George's graveyard proved fruitless.

10

The Scandal of the Dering Roll, 1629

On 4 October 1928, a public auction took place in Ashford of 158 lots comprising the freehold and ancient domain of Surrenden Dering, which included fifteen principal farm holdings producing hops and fruit, including the famous Surrenden hop gardens. Six manor houses including Malmains, Sheerland, Roting and the principal manor of Surrenden Dering were also listed. The area covered holdings in the parishes of Pluckley, Little Chart, Egerton, Hothfield, Westwell and Bethersden. Among the Pluckley businesses and shops on offer were the baker, butcher, wheelwright, blacksmith, post office, school and an engineering workshop.

Surrenden Dering had for nearly 500 years been the ancestral home of the Dering family. The estate covered an area of 3,184 acres (5 square miles) in and around Pluckley, 5 miles to the west of Ashford. The manor house of Surrenden Dering was on an eminence of the greensand ridge, 300ft above sea level, with magnificent views over the Weald to the south and Charing Hill and the North Downs to the north.

The auction catalogue contained a mine of historical information tracing the manor of Pluckley back to Anglo-Saxon times when it belonged to the See of Canterbury. However, after the Conquest, Archbishop Lanfranc granted Pluckley to John Folet in 1070. He was an Anglo-Saxon, and immediately changed his name to de Pluckley. It was common practice at this time for grantees of important manors to link their name to the manor's.

The grantee, as the archbishop's agent, had to provide the king with a specified number of fighting men each year in return for his manorial grant. These fighting men were known as *miles archiepi* – knights of the archbishop. This system was abolished in 1660.

In the early part of the thirteenth century, a de Pluckley descendant died without male issue and so Pluckley was divided between three female co-heirs and the estate was divided into three parts, the manors of Shurland (now called Sheerland), Malmains and Pluckley. Agnes, the co-heir who inherited the redefined Pluckley, had married John Surrenden, and so the manor passed to their son, Richard, who in 1371 built a fine new mansion house that he named Surrenden and this became the name of the downsized Pluckley estate. Malmains and Shurland continued as separate manors for the time being.

Then, once again, a lack of male heirs caused the estate to change family ownership when John Surrenden, the grandson, was succeeded by a daughter, his only offspring, who married John Hart in 1397. The manor passed to him. When he died in 1431, he was survived by an only daughter, Christian, whose husband was John Dering of Lydd. Their son, Richard Dering, was the beneficiary.

Thus began nearly 500 years of the Derings occupying Surrenden Dering, as it eventually became known. In that time, the Derings managed to repatriate the manors of Malmains (sixteenth century) and Sheerland (eighteenth century) into the Surrenden estate as well as adding the manors of Rooting in 1570 and Pivington in 1612, so that by 1928 the Surrenden estate encompassed the entire eastern half of the Weald of Kent.

At the time of the 1928 auction, the Surrenden Dering mansion had twelve principal bedrooms and dressing rooms, and seven reception rooms including a magnificent ballroom and a famous library. Special mention was made in the catalogue of the double avenue of stately elms that was three-quarters of a mile in length and led southwards to St Nicholas's Church, in the village of Pluckley, guarded at each end by picturesque stone entrance lodges. The heavily timbered and undulating deer park running northward down to Little Chart was also of special mention.

The Surrenden Dering mansion's Elizabethan style was designed by the 1st Baronet Sir Edward Dering (1598–1644), who greatly updated and extended Richard Surrenden's original 1371 manor house. A century later, further improvements were made by the 5th Baronet, another Sir Edward Dering, who, in the eighteenth century, extended the mansion and enclosed the whole estate with a brick wall, which is extant today.

1st Baronet Sir Edward Dering.

Sir Edward Dering, 1st Baronet, was without doubt the most illustrious and controversial member of the Dering dynasty, being a man of many parts: courtier, politician, religious controversialist and noted and important antiquarian. His library of manuscripts, maps and book was one of the finest in England and included the earliest surviving manuscript of a Shakespeare play, *Henry VI, Part 1*.

Sir Edward was born in 1598 in the Tower of London, where his father was temporarily lieutenant. He was educated at Westminster School and Magdalene College Cambridge. In 1619, at the age of 21, he married Elizabeth Tufton, a neighbour from Hothfield, whose father, 1st Baronet Sir John Tufton, was influential in Court circles (Sir John died in 1624 and was succeeded by his son, Nicholas, who was created Earl of Thanet in 1629). By this time, Edward Dering was also moving in court circles, his progress being greatly helped by his influential in-laws.

Elizabeth Dering died in 1623 after four years of marriage and in 1625 Edward secured a most advantageous union with Anne Ashburnham, whose family were closely connected to the Duke of Buckingham, a favourite of Charles I. It was not long until, with his father-in-law's influence, Edward Dering was made a baronet in 1627 – not quite a peer but definitely one of the gentry. His quest for nobility was bearing fruit, particularly when he was appointed Lieutenant of Dover Castle, a post that made him the local deputy to the Lord Warden of the Cinque Ports.

In 1628, Sir Edward's second wife, Anne, died after three years of marriage. Once again, he turned this temporary domestic inconvenience to his advantage by marrying for a third time, barely a year later. This time, the bride brought a dowry of £2,000 with her, which helped to clear the debts accumulated from what had turned out to be a disastrous Dover lieutenancy.

In 1629 he was elected MP for Hythe. He was chosen to represent Kent in the Long Parliament from 1640–42 during the English Civil War. This was to prove his downfall. As the historian Arthur Mee so aptly put it, 'He was a man of both sides, wanting reform but not quite a Puritan, seeking peace with the King but not quite a Royalist'.

Sir Edward presented to Parliament the so-called Root and Branch Petition of 1641, whose purpose was to curb the powers and flummery of the bishops, which greatly upset Charles I. In an abrupt volte-face to make amends, Sir Edward presented a contrary petition, which naturally upset Cromwell's Purists. He even involved his neighbour from Bethersden, Richard Lovelace. As a result, they were both imprisoned by Cromwell.

The Dering Roll.

Dering's newly furnished mansion was plundered on four occasions by Cromwell's soldiers. Legend has it that one of his family escaped through an arch-shaped window that was later immortalised in the nineteenth century by a Dering descendant, who fitted similar windows to all estate dwellings. Sir Edward's estates were confiscated, and he spent his last days living in one of his estate cottages in relative poverty.

However, his enduring legacy was the vast library he amassed, the most important item being the Dering Roll, which contained the coats of arms of all the important families in Kent and Sussex (324 in all) in the thirteenth century. It was commissioned by Stephen of Penchester when he was the Constable of Dover Castle from 1268–99. It is 8ft 6in long and 8¼in wide and contains a quarter of the English baronage at the time of Edward I. Dering acquired it during his time as Lieutenant of Dover Castle in 1629.

However, it contains one gigantic flaw. In his quest for nobility at any price, Sir Edward Dering replaced one of the coats of arms with the Dering shield and the false name Richard Fitz-Dering, a fictitious ancestor from Anglo-Norman times. (This was the proud claim of all noble families, a lineage traceable to those days.) Today, the Dering Roll resides in the British Library, saved for the nation at a cost of £194,000 in 2007. Sir Edward's son, Edward, the 2nd Baronet, was able to reclaim the estate and, by the time Charles II acceded to the throne, the Dering Estate was fully restored.

The 3rd Baronet, yet another Edward (1650–89), was commissioned by King William and Queen Mary to raise one of twenty-five regiments to resist the attempts by James II to win back the throne from his new stronghold in Ireland. It is remarkable that Sir Edward, a civilian with little or no military experience, was commissioned a colonel in charge of 900 officers and men.

Thus, was born in April 1689, the 24th Foot Regiment. It fought with great distinction in Ireland, but Sir Edward died of a fever in September 1689. His brother Richard assumed command of the 24th and helped defeat James II at the Battle of the Boyne in 1690. He also succumbed to a fever in 1691.

The 24th Foot Regiment became the Royal Regiment of Wales in a 1969 amalgamation and in 1989, Pluckley celebrated the 24th's tricentennial with a service at St Nicholas's Church attended by the High Sheriff of Kent and the commanding officer of its successor regiment, the Royal Regiment of Wales.

The 8th Baronet Sir Edward Cholmeley Dering (1807–96) inherited the title at the age of 4 and held it for eighty-five years. It was he who installed the arch-shaped windows throughout the Dering estate to celebrate a Dering family member's escape from Cromwell's troops in 1640. This was Victorian romanticism undoubtedly, but, with hindsight, can be seen as an act of profligacy that was to be a serious factor – combined with poor management and gambling debts – in Dering's financial downfall.

In 1906, the 10th Baronet Sir Henry Dering inherited a practically bankrupt estate. He endeavoured to keep Surrenden afloat by selling bits and pieces of the estate, but to no avail. However, by 1928, he was forced to sell to intermediaries, who quickly put the estate up for auction. Much of the estate was bought by the tenants and Surrenden Dering Manor was sold to a Mr Winter, who turned the mansion into a fine preparatory school, Northlaw, which in 1953 was largely destroyed by an accidental fire. All that remains today is the service wing, or east wing, and the stables and coach house, both built by the 5th Baronet in the eighteenth century.

The remains of the north wing of Surrenden Dering.

The remains of the stable block.

Sadly, nothing survives of the original mansion, built by Sir Edward Dering (1598–1644) a century earlier. However, the ubiquitous Dering windows, added in the late-nineteenth century, can be seen today in many buildings in the Pluckley area. A grateful descendant in the nineteenth century had all the windows of the estate changed to an inverted U-shape as it was through such a window that a member of the Dering family escaped from Cromwell's troops during the 1640s. They were installed in all properties owned by the Dering family in Pluckley and the surrounding villages.

The Derings' connection with St Nicholas's Church, Pluckley, meant that it, like so many churches near a great manor, effectively became a private memorial to the noble family.

Also surviving is the Derings' hunting lodge, built in the 1840s next to Pluckley Railway Station to accommodate guests from London down for a weekend of sport. It is a replica of the main manor house, only on a smaller scale, featuring the impressive Dutch gables. It has for over 100 years been an inn called the Dering Arms and, under the same ownership since 1984, it has developed a fine reputation as one of Kent's finest seafood restaurants.

The Dering Arms.

The first Dering to live at Surrenden was John, whose wife was buried at St Nicholas's Church in the south chancel. This was rebuilt by her son Richard and all subsequent Derings have been buried here. Many of them have brass memorials and others have sculptured images. St Nicholas's, the repository of the Dering legacy, is immortalised along with Pluckley village and the surrounding countryside in the hugely successful 1990 television adaptation of H.E. Bates's novel *The Darling Buds of May*, starring David Jason and a young Catherine Zeta-Jones.

St Nicolas's Church has close links to the Dering family.

* * *

Pluckley and the Derings have a 500-year association, so it would be hard to believe that Pluckley's reputation as the most haunted village in Britain had no Dering associations. Of the twelve identified ghosts, four have Dering links.

The Red Lady, a Lady Dering, was buried in the family vault in St Nicholas's Church, along with a red rose, but she is forever searching for the baby she lost at birth, both inside the church and in the graveyard.

Another Lady Dering, the Red Lady's mother or sister, known as the White Lady, haunts the Surrenden Dering Mansion because her husband, in a somewhat macabre act, hoped to preserve her beautiful countenance by encasing her in three lead coffins so that he could gaze upon her beauty at will. Her ghost haunts the mansion, seeking a proper burial at St Nicholas's.

The Lady of Rose Court was a Dering mistress who committed suicide and now haunts Rose Court.

11

Richard Lovelace: The Cavalier Poet, 1642

One of the most romantic and yet tragic figures in English literature must be the so-called 'Cavalier Poet', Richard Lovelace. He was born in Woolwich, Kent, in 1618, the son of Sir William Lovelace and descended from an ancient and distinguished Kentish family which had held the manor of Bethersden near Ashford since 1367. The family prospered greatly between the fourteenth and fifteenth centuries in industry and commerce, and were founder members of the Virginia Company, whose purpose was to assist the colonisation and expansion of America.

Richard Lovelace.

Richard Lovelace's great-grandfather was William Lovelace, Sergeant at Law (a senior-class barrister from whom judges were chosen). He was Member of Parliament for Canterbury in 1562 and 1572, and when he died in 1577 he was buried in the nave of Canterbury Cathedral. It was he who purchased the ancient site of Grey Friars in Canterbury.

From the root in Bethersden there grew, in Kent, the Kingsdown,

Grey Friars, Canterbury.

Hever (both now in West Kingsdown), Sittingbourne and Canterbury Lovelace branches, and in Berkshire, the Hurley branch, which became the seat of the Barons of Hurley. Mention is made of these diversifications because it explains the confusion that has often been caused to historians, including Edward Hasted, in correctly identifying the family's ancestors.

Richard Lovelace was the eldest of eight children and his mother Anne was the daughter of Sir William Barnes of Woolwich who, like Richard's father, was a member of the colonising Virginia Company. In 1602, both his father and grandfather were serving officers with the English forces in Holland and, in 1628, when Richard was only 10 years old, his father died on active service. His grandfather, Sir William the Elder, survived his own son by a year, and although he lived at the family's Grey Friars home in Canterbury, he chose to be buried in the south chapel at St Margaret's Church in Bethersden, where many of his ancestors were also buried. Richard Lovelace spent much of his childhood at his grandfather's home at Grey Friars on the banks of the Stour, and no doubt drew inspiration from this idyllic setting for his later poems.

His mother remarried not long after his father's death, and she and her new husband, Jonathan Brown of London, a Doctor of Law, brought up Richard and his seven brothers and sisters. Sadly, his mother died in 1633 when Richard was 15 years old, but his stepfather and Uncle Miles Barnes MA were appointed joint trustees to administer Anne's estate until Richard Lovelace became of age. He was, at the time of his mother's death, attending Charterhouse School and later matriculated to Gloucester Hall (now Worcester College) Oxford.

It was at Oxford that he began to make a dramatic impact on those around him. In the words of Anthony Wood in his rather sketchy 1691 entry in *Athenae Oxoniensis*:

> Lovelace was then accounted the most amiable and beautiful person that eye could ever behold; a person of innate modesty and virtue and courtly deportment which made him then, but especially after when he retired to the great city, much admired and adored by the female sex.

During the first two years of his time at Oxford he produced his first published writings, including *The Scholar*, which was performed to great applause in Oxford and London. He also began writing poetry, which he contributed to the *Musarum Oxensiensium Charisteria*.

It was small wonder that in 1636 our Adonis was presented to King Charles I and Queen Henrietta when they were on a visit to Oxford. The agent in this matter was a 'great lady' attached to the Court of Henrietta, who recommended to the Chancellor of the University, Archbishop Laud, that Lovelace be granted the degree of Master of Arts after only two years' study (a process which normally took six years).

Leaving Oxford in 1638, he 'repaired in great splendour to the Royal Court', but soon sought active employment in the profession of arms. Under the patronage of the Earl of Norwich, Lord Goring, he went as an ensign (the lowest form of commissioned officer) on the first Scottish Expedition in 1639. On the second expedition, he was commissioned as captain and at that time wrote a tragedy called *The Soldier*. However, it is sad to record that none of his plays are extant.

After the pacification of Berwick, Lovelace, being over 21, returned to Kent to claim his inheritance, which included property at Bethersden, Great Chart, Shaddoxhurst, Halden and Grey Friars in Canterbury, together with an income of at least £500 a year. He immediately immersed himself in local affairs and became involved in the great national issue of the day, the struggle between king and Parliament.

He was a committed Royalist and was put on the Commission of Peace for the county. It is at this point that his characteristic insouciance was to undermine his otherwise charmed life. Part of the blame for his carelessness must rest with his somewhat eclectic neighbour, Sir Edward Dering of Pluckley, whom we met in Chapter 10. In 1641, he was the leading Kentish MP in the Long Parliament. You will remember that he presented the 'Root and Branch' petition of 1641 which upset Charles I and, to make amends, he then presented a seemingly contrary petition, which instead upset the reforming Puritan majority. The Kentish petition was considered seditious and was ordered to be burnt by the hands of the common hangman.

Unwisely, Lovelace allowed himself to be persuaded by Dering to have another 'go', and on 28 April 1641, he had the temerity to present to both Houses of Parliament a similar Kentish petition to restore the king to his rights. Oliver Cromwell and his fellow Puritans acted with typical ruthlessness and Lovelace was imprisoned in the Gatehouse, Westminster. After seven weeks' confinement he was released on bail for the sum of £4,000 on condition that he did not leave the London area without a pass from the Speaker. During his confinement he is said to have written the immortal poem that contained the well-known lines:

Stone walls do not a Prison make,
Nor iron bars a Cage,
Mindes innocent and quiet take
That for an Hermitage.

As a result of his conditional bail, Lovelace remained in London for several months. He lived expensively and greatly enjoyed the wit and companionship of all the great writers and musicians of the day. Also, for a 24-year-old, the attractions of the London social scene were irresistible with its cornucopia of fine wines, food and elegant ladies! It was probable at this time that he met the love of his life, the beautiful Lucy Sacheverell, whose family were very important on the political scene, emanating from an ancient Midlands family from Derbyshire and Warwickshire.

He spent the greater part of the years 1642–47 in Holland and France, initially in the train of his old commander, Lord Goring. During this time, he was secretly furnishing his younger brothers, Francis, William and Dudley, with vast sums of money and men for the king's cause. William was killed at Carmarthen in 1645, and shortly after, Richard returned from abroad and joined King Charles in Oxford. This was to no avail because Charles surrendered in 1646.

Richard Lovelace returned to the Continent, where he raised a regiment for the service of France, which was then at war with Spain. He was its colonel and, with his brothers Dudley and Francis alongside him, he helped capture Dunkirk. During this period, he wrote his famous poem dedicated to Lucasta on 'Going to the Wars', which commences with the memorable lines:

Tell me not (sweet) I am unkind
That from the nunnerie
Of thy chaste breast and quiet mind
To warre and arms I flie.

Lucasta was almost certainly Lucy Sacheverell, and it was during the capture of Dunkirk in 1646 that she heard a strong report that Richard Lovelace had perished. Soon after, she married another and our hero was devastated.

On his return to England in 1647, Lovelace was arrested and committed to Petre House in Aldersgate Street, London, which was then used for the detention of political prisoners. He was released in 1649 and in the same year he published a volume of his poems dedicated to the 'Rt Hon. My Lady Anne Lovelace', wife of his kinsman, the 2nd Lord Lovelace of Hurley. They were collected under the title of *Lucasta* and one of his poems contains the words 'To Lucasta from Prison', a sad reference to the true object of his affections, Lucy Sacheverell:

Long in they shackles liberty
I ask not from these walls but thee
Left fore awhile anothers bride
To fancy all the world beside.

After the execution of Charles I in January 1649, Lovelace was released and suffered the ignominy of having to sell the manor of Lovelace, Bethersden, and other properties to pay the huge debts that he had accumulated in the cause of recklessly supporting his sovereign. He had now lost everything; not only his estates but also the object of his affections, Lucy Sacheverell.

St Margaret's Church in Bethersden.

The last eight years of Richard Lovelace's life were spent in relative obscurity, moving continuously from one lodging house to another around the Fetter Lane area of London. As a prominent Royalist, he was constantly harassed by Cromwell's Parliamentarians and was often forced into hiding. He was well supported by friends, but the strain of his stressful situation took its toll, culminating in his premature death from consumption in 1657, aged 39. He was buried at the west end of St Bride's Church, which was one of the churches that burnt in the Great Fire of London in 1666.

At the time of his death, he was in the process of preparing a second volume of his poems for publication. He did not live to see the book through the press. The work of editing *Lucasta Posthume Poems* was carried out by his youngest brother, Dudley, and was finally published in 1660.

Interestingly, there is no proof that Richard Lovelace ever married, and the daughter, Margaret, ascribed to him by certain historians was in fact his father's cousin, the daughter of Richard Lovelace of Kingsdown (Reverend A.J. Pearman – *Archaeologia Cantianai, Vol. 10*).

It would be difficult to express in poetry, no matter how well endowed with pathos, the tragedy of Richard Lovelace's own life. And what of his younger brothers?

Francis had a glittering diplomatic career in espionage, acting as a conduit between Charles II, while exiled in France, and Cromwell, and also the colony of Virginia. After the restoration of the monarchy in 1660, he eventually became the second Governor of New York (1667–73). His other brothers, Dudley and Thomas, supported Francis in his adventures in the New World. However, it is sad to record that none of his five brothers had legitimate issue.

12

The Father of Electricity and his Ecclesiastical Helper, 1729

In July 1729, two of the most unlikely amateur Kent scientists demonstrated in the most dramatic fashion that static electricity could be transmitted across large distances (conduction) and therefore harnessed for large-scale practical purposes. Until then, static electricity, which had been known about since the time of the Greek philosopher Plato, had largely been used as a phenomenon for public entertainment in theatres, coffee houses and society weddings.

Stephen Gray (1666–1736).

The two self-taught scientists were as different as chalk and cheese. One was a 63-year-old impecunious, retired dyer called Stephen Gray (1666–1736). He was an amateur astronomer of some distinction who was also delving into the mysteries of electrical conduction. He was probably educated at one of the basic petty or elementary schools that were springing up at this time. The other was a 28-year-old aristocratic clergyman, the Reverend Granville Wheler (1701–71), who graduated from Christ's College Cambridge, where he was a Fellow from 1722–24. He purchased Otterden Place, near Charing in Kent, from his brother's widow in 1724, the year he married Lady Maria, the daughter of the 7th Earl of Huntingford, by whom he had seven children. Otterden Place was set in 200 acres of parkland and was the ideal place for Gray to undertake his experiments in conducting static electricity over long distances.

Gray and Wheler realised that a bit of show business was required to draw attention to their ground-breaking experiments in the conduction of electricity. So, an 8-year-old boy was suspended in mid-air by silk threads which acted as insulators, so that they could pass the static electricity from a jar, through the boy, literally from his toes to his hands. A volunteer touched the boy's hand and received a shock, which produced a dramatic spark for all to see. Gray and Wheler then went on to transmit electricity over distances of more than 800ft across the grounds of Otterden Place.

Stephen Gray was apprenticed to his father as a trainee dyer on leaving elementary school. In his spare time, he became interested in astronomy in which he gained much knowledge and achievements; so much so that he came to the attention of the first Astronomer Royal, John Flamsteed, who was in the process of building the Greenwich Observatory. He invited Gray to Greenwich for several months to assist in the creation of the famous observatory. He took young Gray under his wing and introduced him to Henry Hunt, a minor functionary of the Royal Society and Head of Gresham College, who taught Gray much and also published Gray's own papers.

By the time he was 40, Gray was a well-respected astronomer and Roger Coles, a protégé of Sir Isaac Newton, invited him to Cambridge to assist in setting up a new observatory, which sadly ended in failure. He returned to Canterbury, but a bad back made it impossible for him to continue his trade as a dyer. He appealed to the Secretary of the Royal Society to intercede for him with the governors of the Charterhouse to become one of the eighty gentlemen pensioners.

Eventually, in 1719, on the nomination of the Prince of Wales, Gray became a Charterhouse gentleman pensioner. He was able to carry out his experiments in astronomy and electricity in comparative security without the worry of how he was going to keep a roof over his head and eat. This whole episode demonstrates the high regard with which he was held in the scientific community.

However, constant disagreements between Gray's sponsor, Flamsteed, and Sir Isaac Newton, President of the Royal Society, delayed Gray's admission

Otterden Place.

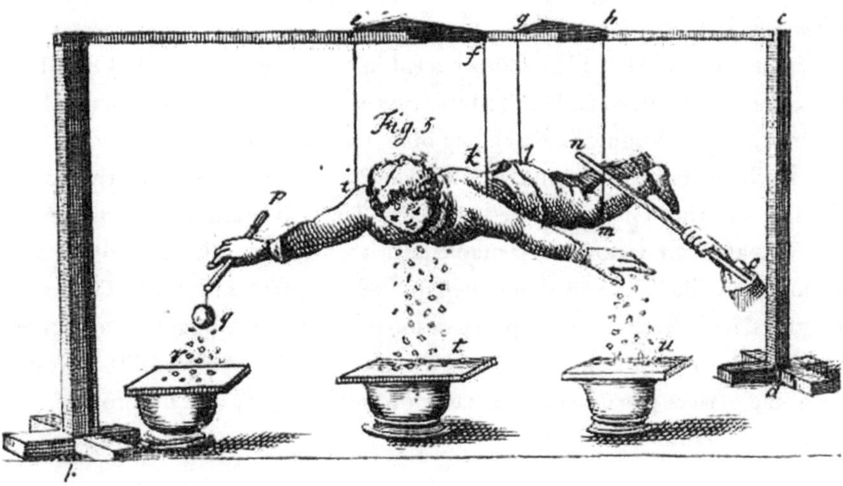

The famous 'suspended boy'.

into the Royal Society. But after he won the prestigious Copley Medal for scientific achievement in 1731 and 1732, he was, in 1732, admitted to the Royal Society as an honorary member.

Stephen Gray died four years later in 1736 and while on his death bed, he asked the secretary of the Royal Society to visit him. He confided the secrets of his experiments to him. He had given to future generations one of the greatest inventions the world has ever known. He harnessed electricity so that it could be used in communication, lighting, power and air conditioning, both domestic and industrial. And it will soon completely replace the internal combustion engine to power motor vehicles.

Sadly, there is no monument to Stephen Gray and even the whereabouts of his grave is uncertain, although he is believed to be buried in a common grave in an old London cemetery in an area reserved for pauper pensioners from the Charterhouse. However, in 2017, the School of Physical Sciences at the University of Kent in Canterbury initiated the Stephen Gray Lectures in his memory.

And what of Gray's young protégé, the Reverend Granville Wheler, who had been elected to the Royal Society in 1728, at the age of 27, four years before Gray and a year before their ground-breaking experiments in 1729? He published his own observations as to the repulsive power of electricity in *Philosophical Transactions* in 1739.

He died on 12 May 1770 and is buried in St Laurence Church, Otterden, which he had designed and built a few years earlier. The locals had viewed him with a certain amount of fear, calling him 'The Wizard'.

The Wheler family occupied Otterden Place until 2004 when the last in the line, another Granville, died childless. Today, Otterden Place is part of the Wheler Foundation, a charitable trust that includes the Ledston Estate, which Granville Wheler had inherited in 1789 through his first wife, Catherine Hastings. Its objectives are the preservation of historic buildings and landscapes and the education of children about the countryside. Otterden Place would seem the perfect place to erect a statue of Stephen Gray and his protégé, the Reverend Granville Wheler.

13

The Ingoldsby Legends, 1837

The Ingoldsby Legends were first published in 1837 and represent a style of writing described as being characterised by their grotesque treatment of medieval legends, with lively rhythms and inventive rhymes. They were an early precursor of the work of W.S. Gilbert in his Savoy Operas with Arthur Sullivan, and were much quoted by other writers, such as H.G. Wells, Henry James (*Ghost Stories*) and H. Rider Haggard (*King Solomon's Mines*).

The legends first appeared in *Bentley's Miscellany* in 1837 and were written, apparently, by Thomas Ingoldsby, which is the *nom de plume* of the Reverend Richard Barham. They were illustrated by John Leech and George Cruikshank, who both illustrated Charles Dickens's work. Due to their immense popularity, they were collected into book form in 1840. They are now reduced to cult status, having been overtaken by other writers who adopted their style and expanded their range of humour.

One of the most quoted sections of one of his most famous poems is from 'The Leech of Folkestone':

> The world according to the best geographers is divided into Europe, Asia, Africa, America and Romney Marsh.
>
> In this, the fifth, quarter of the globe, a witch may still be occasionally discovered in favourable, i.e. stormy, season, weathering Dungeness point in an eggshell, or careering on her broomstick over Dymchurch wall.

A major reason why the Reverend Barham didn't feature in the mainstream of literature was due to his profession as a cleric. His style of writing was not in keeping with a minor canon of St Paul's Cathedral and a Priest in Ordinary to the Chapel Royal, serving the Royal Household at Hampton Court and St James's Palace. His fertile mind and felicity for writing comic verse was apparent from an early age and it is here we must start.

Richard Harris Barham the Younger was born on 6 December 1788 at 61 Burgate, Canterbury. His father was of the same name and his mother was Richard Barham Senior's housekeeper, Elizabeth Fox. There is no evidence that mother and father had ever married, so young Richard was illegitimate – a very progressive situation for an Alderman and Mayor of Canterbury!

The Barham family were able to trace their ancestry back to William the Conqueror and the Fitz Urses, who came over from Normandy in 1066. They were granted lands in what became the Manor of Barham, south of Canterbury in the Elham Valley, along which flows the Little Stour to Canterbury. It was one of the Barham ancestors, at the time of Henry II, who, with three other knights, murdered Thomas Becket on 29 December 1170 in Canterbury Cathedral. He fled to Ireland in disgrace and in recognition, the family changed their name from Fitz Urse to de Barham, after their manor. This was eventually shortened to Barham.

It's small wonder that young Richard Barnham had such a fertile imagination, and he also inherited his father's genial nature, but not his appetite for food and drink, which had caused his father to tip the scales at 27 stone at the time of his death at the early age of 48 in 1795. He bequeathed to his son the Manor of Barham and more particularly, the farmhouse known as 'Tappington', which was to be the inspiration for *The Ingoldsby Legends*, with the focal point being the fictitious house of Tappington Everard.

At the time of his father's death, Richard was barely 7 years old, with a mother who was of a poor constitution. Therefore, three guardians were appointed to supervise the boy's welfare including Lord Rokesby and a somewhat dodgy attorney. After a period of home tuition, he was sent off, at the age of 9, to St Paul's School in London. The High Master, Dr Roberts, and his wife became surrogate parents.

At St Paul's he made many friends including Richard Bentley, who was later to be his publisher. But in 1802, when he was 14, tragedy struck when the Dover Mail, returning him to school from Canterbury, overturned and crushed his arm and took him to death's doorstep. The fact that he recovered is in no small way due to the ministrations of Mrs Roberts, the High Master's wife. So serious had young Barham's condition been at one time that his

Richard Barham.

Tappington Everard.

guardians had, with great asperity, put matters in hand for the disposal of his Barham estates.

In life, it is often the case that from unfortunate circumstances arise opportunities that are a seminal influence on the course of one's life. In this case, during young Barham's convalescence, Mrs Roberts allowed him to attend her literary gatherings, to foster the literary talent which he undoubtedly had, including advice from a dramatic actress of some note, Sarah Bartley, who gave him instruction on the art of delivering what he had composed – Dickens style. Even the irrefragable High Master Roberts fanned the flame by employing young Barham to write speeches, not only for himself but also for the other boys. In 1807, a selection of the schoolboy compositions was published and received favourable reviews in the *Gentleman's Magazine* for a precocious talent which displayed much promise of future excellence.

The Dark Entry at Canterbury Cathedral.

In the same year, as his first venture into the printed word, he went up to Brasenose College Oxford, where he initially got in with 'the wrong set' (to quote Evelyn Waugh) and this led to a somewhat wild and extravagant undergraduate life, including heavy gambling losses. His guardians refused to pay these debts. However, one of their number, Lord Rokesby, gave Barham the money as a friend – he would not lend it. This so impressed Barham that he changed his way of life, obtained his BA degree in law and returned home to Canterbury.

In 1813 his mother died, and to compound matters, he became seriously ill. It was during his recovery period that he first entertained the notion of becoming a candidate for Holy Orders and in that same year was duly ordained. The following year, he was appointed curate in the village of Westwell and married

Caroline Smart, the daughter of Captain Smart of the Royal Engineers. Of this union were born two boys, one of whom died in infancy in 1817.

The family lived in the Parsonage, which was situated in the appropriately named Watery Lane, a decidedly unhealthy location that undoubtedly contributed to his youngest son's early demise. There is a tablet in Westwell Church commemorating the infant's death. Shortly afterwards, the Archbishop appointed Barham Rector of Snargate and at the same time, he appointed him to the curacy of Warehorne. The former was placed firmly in Romney Marsh and the latter, on the edge.

It was in this unique part of the world – in the centre of the 'free trade' (smuggling) – that his imagination was given free rein. His parishioners were, to a man, wholly engaged in the illicit trade, and it required considerable tact on his part to gain acceptance and trust from his 'free-trading' parishioners. On misty nights on the eerie Marsh, long lines of mounted smugglers passed by with horses laden with contraband on their way to the church, where the consignments of lace, brandy and tobacco were stored in the Snargate belfry. The nightly wage paid to the participants was 7*s* 6*d* for an unarmed smuggler and 15*s* to those who carried cutlass and pistols.

The residents of Romney Marsh, on the face of things, lacked the intellectual intercourse so desired by writers, but their 'free trade' activity provided inspiration for some of his most memorable literary work. Due to another accident in which he broke a leg overturning the gig on the way to Ashford, he was confined to the vicarage for some weeks. It was during this period of inactivity and convalescence that he wrote his first novel, *Baldwin*, and the opening chapters of his second novel, *My Cousin Nicholas*. (*Baldwin* sadly fell, stillborn, from the press.)

Kipling's atmospheric 'A Smugglers Song' encapsulates the ethos of the community in which he lived:

Five and twenty ponies trotting through the dark
Brandy for the Parson, Baccy for the Clerk
Laces for the Lady, Letters for the Spy
Watch the wall my darling while the Gentlemen go by.

Then, in 1817, on a visit to London, he encountered an old friend who told him of a vacancy for a minor canonry at St Paul's Cathedral. He duly applied and was successful. On 6 April 1821 he took up this prestigious appointment in the City of London. In 1824, he was presented with the living of St Mary Magdalene and St Gregory by St Paul's and was made Priest in Ordinary to the Chapel Royal – St James's Palace.

He now found time to write topical and religious articles and poetry, which were published in various periodicals. He met various literary people, including Mrs Hughes, the grandmother of Thomas Hughes, author of *Tom Brown's Schooldays*, the result being that he finished *My Cousin Nicholas*, which was published in parts in 1834 in *Blackwood's Magazine* and was a great success. However, when it was issued as a book it was not such a success.

Novel writing was a literary form that Barham did not find easy, unlike verse. The birth of *The Ingoldsby Legends* came about because of his desire to help his old friend, Richard Bentley, who published the first issue of *Bentley's Miscellany* in January 1837, edited by Charles Dickens. Barham adopted the pen name Thomas Ingoldsby in case it was thought unseemly for a minor canon of St Paul's to be the creator of such, as it turned out, anarchic verse.

His first contribution was 'The Spectre of Tappington', the first of many verses concerning his family home. The ideas for more verses were supplied by the fertile mind of Mrs Hughes, who was a veritable mine of ghost stories. The various tales were published under the generic title of *The Ingoldsby Legends* and were a huge success. Readers became curious about their author, but Dickens refused to reveal his true name.

Barham's stories came from all over Kent, not just his ancestral home of Tappington. 'Canterbury Cathedral's Dark Entry' features Nell Cook's ghost; 'The Women in Grey' is a legend of Dover; 'Grey Dolphin' is a tale of Sheppey; and 'Ingoldsby Abbey' is the ruined church of St Mary's, Denton, in Gravesend. In fact, the three volumes contained over sixty stories and were issued from 1840–47. His son, another Reverend Richard Barham, produced the 1847 volume posthumously.

Sadly, in 1840, Barham Senior received a shock from which he never really recovered. His youngest and favourite 12-year-old son died of cholera. It possibly contributed to his own death because a few years later in 1844, when attending the opening of the Royal Exchange, he caught a severe chill from which he never recovered and he died a painful death in June 1845. Typically, as he lay dying, he composed his last poem, 'As I lay A thynkynge'. He was buried in St Mary Magdalene, Old Fish Street Hill, but after a fire in 1886 his remains were translated to Kensal Green Cemetery.

The real Tappington Farm, where Barham resided.

In Canterbury today there are reminders of this unique literary figure: a brass plaque on the side of what was his house in Burgate (61 Burgate was bombed in the Second World War), a memorial bronze plaque in the Guildhall in Canterbury and – the ultimate accolade – a large Wetherspoon's pub called the Thomas Ingoldsby. And, of course, there is Tappington Manor, if you can find it!

14

Lord Harris: The Father of Kent Cricket, 1870

A club representing the county of Kent was first founded in 1842 but Kent teams have played top-class cricket since the early eighteenth century and the club has always held first-class status. However, the representative team was somewhat diluted in strength by the formation of a second county club at Maidstone in 1859.

This was clearly an unsatisfactory situation, and it took the intervention of the 3rd Baron Harris, a great cricket enthusiast, to 'knock heads together', so to speak, and persuade the two disparate clubs to merge in 1870 to form Kent County Cricket Club, with his son, the legendary future 4th Baron Harris, as its captain.

The 4th Baron Harris combined this with the post of honorary secretary until 1889, when he resigned on becoming Governor of Bombay. On his return to the UK in 1895, he took up and resumed his association with Kent as president and later as chairman of the club until his death in 1932. He, more than anybody, guided Kent during its halcyon years 1906–13 when Kent won the County Championship no fewer than four times. Additionally, during his playing days, he became England's second test captain between 1879–84 in four matches against Australia, both home and away.

George Robert Canning Harris was born on 3 February 1851 in Trinidad, where his father, 3rd Baron Harris, was serving as governor until 1854, when the family moved on to Madras. His father was appointed governor there before returning to England on his retirement. He then became involved in Kent County Cricket as a committee member and in 1870 became club president.

Meanwhile, young George Harris attended Eton before going on to Christ Church Oxford from 1871–74, playing cricket for Oxford University as well as Kent. His father died in 1873 and he became the 4th Baron Harris while still an undergraduate at Oxford.

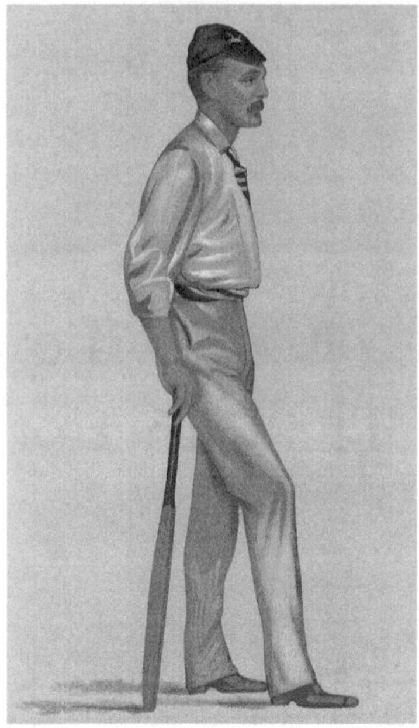

The young 4th Baron, Lord Harris.

After leaving Oxford, Harris was politically active as a member of the Conservative Party, serving in the House of Lords as Undersecretary of State for India and then Undersecretary of State for War, before being appointed Governor of Bombay from 1890–95.

The 4th Baron Harris became an influential figure in cricket administration, both nationally and internationally, through offices he held with the Marylebone Cricket Club (MCC), as trustee and treasurer (1906–32). He was also chairman of the finance and cricket subcommittees and, in 1909, chaired a meeting of representatives of England, Australia and South Africa, which launched the Imperial Cricket Conference. In 1926, Harris chaired a meeting which admitted the West Indies, New Zealand and India to the test-playing fold and made provision for other teams from the Empire to join when they were ready. Sir Charles Igglesden wrote of Lord Harris that 'no man has exercised so strong an influence on the cricket world for so long'.

Harris died in March 1932 aged 82, leaving a widow, Lucy, whom he had married in 1874, and a son, who succeeded to the barony as the 5th Baron Harris. That great authority on Kent cricket, Sir Charles Igglesden, editor of the *Kentish Express,* paid a very fulsome tribute to the 4th Baron Harris in his book, *66 Years' Memories of Kent Cricket*, published in 1946 and I can do no better than to quote from it verbatim:

The name of the late Lord Harris will always be associated with Kent cricket. For years he nursed it, and the child grew and grew under his care until Kent became recognised as one of the leading counties, The love of the game ran riot in his veins. He first played for Kent in 1870, and his highest score was 176 against Sussex at Gravesend; his last year was 1911. For five years he was Governor-General of Bombay, but his love of cricket never deserted him. The game had been played by Englishmen in that part of the world, but on his initiative it spread to the high-class natives, and as we saw in 1946 a wonderful team came to England. Previously Ranjitsinhji, and Indian Prince, came here and became famous as a batsman. As a stylish batsman could Lord Harris be described. He broke down the prejudice against the recognised rule that only during Canterbury Week did amateurs play in the Kent county team. It was during the Week that Lord Harris played his last match in 1911, and he received a terrific ovation as he came out of the pavilion to bat. Not only from the West Indian eleven but from all around the ground the cheers from thousands of throats resounded as men and women stood up. The wicket was a cranky one, but the veteran cricketer, from the first ball he received until the last, showed his old style. He scored 33.

While in Bombay Lord Harris wrote to me, 'I am trying my best to become enthusiastic about cricket out here, but I dream of matches on our Kent grounds. And when those dreams came true what joy!'

It was Lord Harris who first introduced covering a wicket when rain was falling, and he went so far as to express an opinion that it would be a good plan to cover the whole ground at the same time, but admitted that it would not only be a costly innovation but would take too much time, and the ground might be soaked by a shower before the cover was completed.

One of the most difficult decisions to be made by umpires is the question of stopping play owing to bad light. Lord Harris told me that on one occasion in India he was fielding at mid-off in a bad light owing to the glare of the sun, but the batsman objected to the drawing of stumps. Presently came a catch to his Lordship, with the sun full in his face. He realised that it was coming straight to his face. In self-protection he threw up his hand, saw nothing but found the ball in one hand. 'The best catch I ever made,' he said afterwards.

What a grand gift was Lord Harris, not merely to Kent but to the world of cricket in general. He had the reputation of being a despot in the field. This may have been the case, but he was fair-minded and especially encouraging

4th Baron, Lord Harris.

The St Lawrence Ground, home of Kent Cricket Club.

to the young and nervous player. Well do I remember a catch being dropped by a young professional in his first match at Canterbury. For a moment his lordship showed irritation, for Shrewsbury's wicket was worth taking. At the luncheon interval I was talking to the Kent captain when he beckoned to the disconsolate colt. From his pocket he took one of those glittering sovereigns which we never see today, and placed it in the youngster's hand. 'Sorry I swore about that catch,' he said. 'A very good try. Better luck next time.' What fine encouragement and what chivalry! I expect Walter Hearne remembered the incident long after he had to retire from active cricket and become Kent's scorer.

I often wonder what would have been the fate of Kent cricket without Lord Harris and George Marsham. I recall one incident. It was a young professional's first appearance for Kent. He played a defensive game, and when he returned to the pavilion was met by Lord Harris and George Marsham. 'Sorry,' said the lad. 'Somehow I felt too shaky to hit out.' 'Don't worry,' said his Lordship. 'A straight bat will always win in the end.' And the young batsman felt two golden sovereigns in the palm of his hand, one from each of the two veterans – Lord Harris and George Marsham. That lad was killed in the last war.

The above is a fitting tribute to a man who contributed more than any other, before or since, not only to the establishment and well-being of cricket in Kent but to cricket throughout the world.

15

Tragic Cuthbert: Kent's Greatest Sporting Icon, 1872

The politician, diplomat and writer C.B. Fry is often acclaimed as England's greatest sporting all-rounder. Another man, however, deserves to rank alongside him in the national sporting pantheon – the Dover-born Cuthbert Ottaway, England's first football captain.

Ottaway achieved this distinction on 30 November 1872, when he captained England against Scotland in the world's first international football match. The game took place at the West of Scotland Cricket Ground, just outside Glasgow, and ended in a 0–0 draw. The author Michael Southwick broke the news with his book, *England's first Football Captain*, in 2009. What he could not have realised when he embarked on his assiduous research was that he would rediscover one of history's greatest all-rounders.

Not long before Ottaway captained England, he had returned from a cricket tour of Canada and the United States with the MCC in which he opened the batting with the legendary W.G. Grace. Earlier that year, Ottaway had represented Oxford University at cricket, football, rackets and real tennis. The next year, he represented Oxford at athletics and in 1874, he captained Oxford University Football Club in their FA Cup final triumph over the Royal Engineers. In total, he represented Oxford University at five sports and made thirteen appearances against Cambridge University – an all-time record for blues-ranked events.

Cuthbert Ottaway.

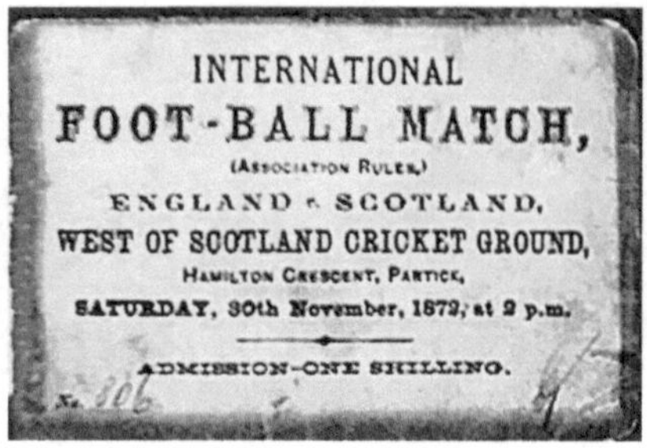

A ticket for the first international football match.

Cuthbert Ottaway was born in Dover at No. 5 Hammond Place, now demolished, near the ruins of St James's Church.

Cuthbert was born in Dover on 18 July 1850, at the family home, No. 5 Hammond Place – long since demolished – a short distance from the old St James's Parish Church where, a year earlier, his parents had married. He was christened there on 14 August. His father, James, was a successful surgeon and his mother was sister of Sir John Bridge, the Bow Street magistrate. James was a pillar of the Dover Establishment: a town councillor, magistrate and mayor in 1859–60. Consequently, Cuthbert's education was a privileged one. He received coaching at a private academy in St James's Street and in 1863 he won a place at Eton as a King's Scholar. By the 1861 census, the Ottaways had moved up in the world, to No. 7 Camden Crescent, overlooking Dover Harbour, three doors away from where Charles Dickens stayed when completing *Bleak House* in 1851 and *Great Expectations* in 1861.

The Ottaway family were men of Kent, through and through, appearing in parish records in three Wealden villages going back to the mid-sixteenth century. They first appear in Bethersden, where Richard Ottaway the Older was born in the 1590s. His son Richard was one of the early pioneers in the New World, reaching North America nearly 250 years before his sporting descendant. He was almost certainly part of the Lovelace family contingent from Bethersden, who went to Virginia and Maryland in the mid-seventeenth century (see Chapter 11 for more on the Lovelaces).

Richard Ottaway died in Maryland in 1666. His son Matthew, born in 1656, moved from Bethersden to nearby Smarden in 1682, when he married Sarah Bunce. Their youngest son Stephen, born in 1696, married Ann Down from nearby Pluckley in 1722. One of their five children was Henry, Cuthbert's great-grandfather, who was a timber merchant in Smarden. One of his children was James, born in Smarden in 1781. He was Cuthbert's grandfather and moved to Staplehurst, where he was married twice and produced three sons and two daughters, including, in 1810, Cuthbert's father, another James.

Grandfather James and his other two sons, Gillett and Philip, were all solicitors, and the young James became a surgeon and moved to Dover when he married Cuthbert's mother. With his thoroughly middle-class pedigree, Cuthbert Ottaway progressed to Eton in 1863 as a King's Scholar, one of only seventy among 1,200 pupils. Not only did King's Scholars have the privilege of living within the school precincts, but they did not have to pay the high fees of the rest, who had to live outside as 'oppidans' – town dwellers.

At Eton, Cuthbert Ottaway was in his element; sporting excellence was the measure of the man and Cuthbert had a natural eye for the ball. It was not

The Ottaways' home,
No. 7 Camden Crescent, Dover.

The Dover Society's
blue plaque.

long before he was representing Eton at rackets – an early form of squash – and fives, similar to rackets but played with a gloved hand instead. He also played the Eton Field Game, one of the many versions of football played at this time. In both 1868 and 1869, he won the Public Schools Rackets Championship.

However, it was cricket at which Cuthbert excelled and he went on to captain Eton against Harrrow at Lord's. This was one of the highlights in the sporting and social calendar and, founded in 1822, is the oldest surviving fixture in cricket. In 1867, he was invited to Lord's for special coaching and represented Eton against the MCC, when he scored an impressive 55 runs.

His final term in 1869 was to be his golden summer. He scored nine centuries, including 108 against Harrow at Lord's. The culmination of this run feast was his selection by his native county, Kent, to play against the mighty MCC, which was captained by W.G. Grace. The match was played at the St Lawrence Ground, Canterbury, and although Kent lost by an innings, Ottaway was Kent's top scorer with 55. It was this performance that paved the way for his selection by the MCC for the 1872 tour of America.

Academically, Ottaway was no slouch, either. In 1869, he won two scholarships from Eton to Brasenose College Oxford, where he studied Classics. I have already mentioned his sporting achievements there, but it was at the newly codified game of Association Football – soccer, for short – that he was to achieve immortality.

Oxford adopted the Cambridge Rules of 1863 that provided a unified code for the various forms of football being played. Oxford University Football Club was founded in November 1871, the same year as the first FA Cup. However, Oxford were founded too late in the season to take part, and so Cuthbert played for Crystal Palace, who reached the semi-finals before losing to the Royal Engineers, who, in turn, lost in the final to the Wanderers. In 1874, Cuthbert captained Oxford when they beat the Royal Engineers in the FA Cup final.

It was in the spring of 1874, having secured a First in Classics, that he left Oxford to pursue his career, starting as a trainee barrister. He was now based in London, and it was natural that he should accept an invitation to join Middlesex, who at this time played at the Prince's Ground in Knightsbridge – they moved to Lord's in 1877.

In the winter, he played football for the Old Etonians, who at their first attempt reached the 1875 FA Cup final, losing to the Royal Engineers 2–0 in a replay. It was Ottaway's third successive FA Cup final and, as it turned out, the last competitive football match in which he played; it ended in a draw, but he injured his ankle so severely in the first game that he could not take part in the replay or any cricket during the 1875 season.

Ottaway was now free to devote himself to his legal studies and gain experience round the courts of London. It was also time for reflection in terms of settling down domestically. No doubt encouraged by his parents, he contacted Marion Stinson, from Hamilton, Ontario, whom he had met and been

The church of St Michael's in Smarden, where Ottaway's ancestors lived for 300 years.

smitten by when he toured Canada with the MCC in 1872. She was now 17, and arrangements were made for Cuthbert to visit Ontario.

The year 1876 was his most successful in cricket: he scored two centuries for Middlesex and finished fourth in the first-class batting averages. After the season's end, he travelled to Ontario to visit Marion and seek her parents' approval for their union. He qualified as a barrister in November 1876, and so the scene was set. On 29 August the following year, Marion and Cuthbert married at Christ Church Cathedral, Ontario. He was 27 and his bride 18.

Although the newlyweds settled down in London where he was now a busy practising barrister, they spent Christmas 1877 with his parents in Dover when it was revealed that Marion was expecting their first child. Sadly, their joy was short-lived.

Late in March 1878, Cuthbert caught a chill after a night's dancing and died from chest complications, possibly tubercular in origin. Cuthbert Ottaway was buried in Paddington Old Cemetery on 2 April and Marion gave birth to their daughter, Lillian, on 22 July 1878.

Marion remained in London for a few years before returning to Canada, where she remarried in 1884 to Patrick Duncan Crerar, a successful lawyer by whom she had three sons and a daughter. She died in 1919, aged 60.

Cuthbert's daughter Lillian had moved to Canada with her mother. An expert horsewoman, she married Sir Adam Beck, a successful businessman and politician, on 7 September 1898. He was 41 and she was 20. In 1904 they had a daughter, Marion. The Becks spent much time in England, particularly during the First World War with the Canadian Red Cross. Lillian died, aged 43, in hospital in Toronto on 17 October 1921, after an operation for pancreatic cancer.

Marion the younger married Strathearn Hay in 1925 and they had a daughter, also Lillian (known as Sally). Marion, like her forebears, died young – at 40, in 1944. Though Sally managed to get through a total of four husbands in a short life (she died in 1969, aged 42), she left only one child, Patricia Broke Bell, from her first marriage to Patrick Broke Bell.

Trish, as she is known, was born in Toronto in 1947 and is alive and well today. She has been married twice and has three children. As of 2009 there are nine living descendants of Cuthbert Ottaway, seven of whom are in Canada and two in the Czech Republic. Look out for the surnames Hunter, Kulchycki and Gaynor in furture sporting annuals: they are great-great-great-great-grandchildren of Cuthbert Ottaway, born between 1998 and 2007.

It was not until the twenty-first century that Cuthbert Ottaway was rediscovered and acclaimed. His neglected grave in Paddington Old Cemetery was restored in 2013, the least that could be done in tribute to the man who is, arguably, Kent's greatest sporting icon.

16

Sir Charles Igglesden: Sauntering Through Kent, 1899

Sir Charles Igglesden, 1928. (National Portrait Gallery)

On 22 April 1899, there appeared in the *Kentish Express*, under the heading 'A Saunter through Kent with Pen and Pencil', an article about Kennington, 'a picturesque parish not two miles distant from Ashford'. The newspaper announced that this was to be the first in a series of articles describing the villages of Kent.

The unnamed author of this first article was Charles Igglesden, the newspaper's editor. The illustrator was Xavier Willis, the *Express's* resident artist. Few could have expected that the series would run for more than forty-five years with the same two wielding pen and pencil. By the time the last feature appeared in October 1944, their peregrinations had covered 242 villages and towns. Such was the demand that the articles were published in hardback book: thirty-four volumes were produced between 1900 and 1946.

The logo for the Saunters Through Kent series, drawn by Xavier Willis.

Henry Igglesden, founder of the *Kentish Express* and father of Charles Igglesden.

Igglesden was appointed editor of the *Kentish Express* in 1884 at the tender age of 23 and served in that post for more than sixty-four years. His peers in Fleet Street and beyond recognised that he was an exceptional journalist and a man of some political acumen, and in 1927 they appointed him president of the Institute of Journalists, the oldest newspaper association in the world. The next year, he was knighted for services to journalism.

However, journalism and the *Saunter* books represented only two facets of his life. His was an eclectic mix of interests and abilities, which included sporting prowess, literary distinction as an author and novelist, archaeology and chess. Above all, he was a politician and man of public affairs who was part of the county's public life for more than half a century. He was an Alderman on Kent County Council for more than forty years and a Deputy Lieutenant of Kent.

Charles Igglesden was born in Ashford on 7 February 1861, the second son of Henry Igglesden, who had founded the *Kentish Express* in 1855. Henry's father, John Bourn Igglesden, was a partner with his brother, Benjamin, in the family bakery business in Market Place, Dover. It had been founded by their father and mother, John and Amy, in 1788. They were a well-respected

Dover family, devout Baptists and a cornerstone of the community. Great-grandfather John had moved to Dover from Benenden in 1730 to pursue a career at sea. However, John Bourn died suddenly, aged 40, in 1836, followed three years later by his wife, Elizabeth.

Henry and his brother George, now orphans, were cared for separately by friends – Henry by John May, a printer, and his wife, Eliza. Henry became apprenticed to John May and once he had completed his indentures he moved to Ashford and married a local girl, Sarah Ann, in 1851, and set up a printing business in the High Street.

In 1855, in the wake of the government's abolition of stamp duty on newspapers, he took a big gamble and founded Kent's first penny newspaper, the *Ashford and Alfred News*. It was published on Saturdays and Tuesdays and, although a risky venture, it paid off handsomely. The '*Alfred*' part of the title related to a new housing development, Alfred Town, built in 1850 by South Eastern Railways for its employees a mile to the east of Ashford, roughly where Willsborough is today.

Henry had perceived that there was a growing demand from an increasingly literate public for news of not only local affairs but also of the wider world. His paper had a Paris newsletter, commentating on events in Europe, and news of parliamentary affairs in London alongside reports on local wheat prices and other farming matters. Such was the widening appeal of the newspaper that it was not long before offices opened in Maidstone, Canterbury, Folkestone and Hastings. In 1858, the *Ashford and Alfred News* became the *Kentish Express* to reflect its wider geographical significance.

Henry and Sarah's third child and second son, Charles, was born at their home in East Hill, Ashford. He had an elder brother and sister, William and Elizabeth, and later another sister, Kate.

Unlike William, Charles did not attend Ashford Grammar School, in the precincts of St Mary's Church in the town centre, because falling numbers had forced the school to shut in 1871. This was no doubt due to the agricultural decline at that time. The school, which had been founded by Sir Norton Knatchbull in 1660, reopened in 1881 in Hythe Road, east Ashford. Today, it is known as the Norton Knatchbull School with more than 1,000 pupils.

As a result of the school's closure, Charles was initially educated at home by tutors. It soon became clear that Charles was extremely gifted academically, particularly in music and literature. He was also an outstanding sportsman, excelling at cricket, tennis and rugby, and receiving coaching at nearby sports clubs. Charles's home tutors also recognised that he was an extremely gifted musician and talented violinist. As a result, he gained entry to the Conservatoire de Paris.

A cosmopolitan education of this sort was most unusual and may have had something to do with the *Kentish Express's* Paris correspondent. Founded in 1795, the Paris Conservatoire also included dance and dramatic declamation in its curriculum and this explains in part Charles's literary leanings. It must be borne in mind that the Royal College of Music in London was not founded until 1882.

Charles returned to England in 1878 and became a cub reporter on his father's paper, taking a special interest in sports reporting, particularly cricket, for which he developed a passion. He was later to write a weekly cricket column under the pen name 'LBW'.

His love of cricket dated back to 1871 when, as a 10-year-old, he attended the world-famous Canterbury Cricket Week and was spotted by the legendary W.G. Grace having a knockabout with some older lads. Using an oak tree as the wicket, W.G. proceeded to give him his first cricket lesson. This was the beginning of a lifelong friendship. In 1876, Charles was lucky enough to witness W.G. scoring 344 sublime runs – the first triple century in first-class cricket – also at Canterbury Cricket Week, playing for the MCC against Kent.

The Canterbury Cricket Week, founded in 1842, is the oldest festival of its type in the world, and Igglesden reported it for more than fifty years. He became an accomplished cricketer himself, playing for several local clubs, and he regularly took teams to play in France up until the First World War.

Charles was a first-class rugby player and represented Kent at lawn tennis, twice being runner up in the County Singles Championship. He was also accomplished at billiards, twice beating Sherlock Holmes's creator, Sir Arthur Conan Doyle, in the final of the Authors Club Championship. In complete contrast, he also represented Kent at chess.

Charles was appointed editor of the *Kentish Express* at the age of 23, ahead of his older brother William, who also worked at the paper, and given his young age, he must have been quite exceptional. The *Express* grew from strength to strength under his editorship, becoming known for its forthright and incisive editorial comments, and by the 1890s attained a circulation of 35,000 a week. His father, Henry, maintained his connection with the paper as chairman until his death in 1907.

In 1891, a disgruntled ex-employee set fire to the *Express* offices and works in Park Street, Ashford, destroying the buildings and every piece of machinery

The former offices and factory of the Kentish Express in Ashford High Street are now a bakery.

and type. A Fleet Street newspaper, the *Daily Chronicle* (later the *News Chronicle*), came to the rescue and printed the *Express* until new premises were built in the High Street a few months later. Amazingly, the paper appeared as usual the next Saturday.

The *Chronicle* was at that stage Fleet Street's biggest-selling newspaper. A few years later, Charles Igglesden was offered the editor's chair at the *Chronicle*, but declined, preferring to stay close to his beloved Kentish countryside. In 1885, he married Ellen, daughter of George E. Swatman, a senior civil servant at the Admiralty. They had four sons, who all worked for the *Kentish Express*.

In 1908, the family moved to Heathfield, an imposing residence on the Canterbury Road, just north of Ashford, and lived there for more than thirty years before Ellen's death in 1939. Charles remained there until he died in 1949. His eldest son, Charles Hubert Igglesden, succeeded his father as editor until his death in 1957. The paper had only three editors in 102 years – and all Igglesdens!

In 1899, Charles wrote *The Demon Eleven*, a collection of short stories about the Canterbury Cricket Week. By 1907, he had also published seven volumes of his *Saunters* and this emboldened him to approach a London firm, Simpkin Marshall, to publish a volume of ten short stories, *Strad*, which received favourable reviews in the national press.

The poet Matthew Arnold once said that journalism was literature in a hurry, and this became the case with Igglesden's literature. In 1910, John Long of London published his first full-length novel, *A Flutter with Fate*, set on Romney Marsh and in Littlestone, followed by three more romantic novels, *Clouds* (1912), which features Hythe, Folkestone and Smeeth; *Law the Wrecker* (1914) and *The Crimson Glow* (1918), set in the North Downs around Charing. A later novel, *Downs Valley Farm* (1940), features the North Downs again, but this time Ashford, Wye and Hastingleigh, and follows the romantic fortunes of two Land Girls posted to the area just after the outbreak of the Second World War.

However, *Those Superstitions*, published in 1931, is his most enduring publication after the *Saunters* series. Clearly, much of the information for this light-hearted investigation into the nature and origins of superstitions was gleaned from his *Saunters* books. It was, however, considered a serious enough work to have been endorsed by the mystery writer Marjorie Bowen, who wrote a lengthy foreword. The book is still held by more than 130 public libraries throughout the world.

Two of Igglesden's books, in addition to the *Saunters* series, were expanded versions of articles that had first appeared in the *Kentish Express* as first-hand reports of official visits made overseas. The first, published in 1916, was entitled *Out There: Impressions of a Visit Under the Auspices of the War Office*. The second book was *A Mere Englishman in America*.

Out There came about partly as a result of an editorial comment that Igglesden had written on 25 September 1915 urging the government to shed more light on what was happening on the Western Front. He likened the government's claim that 'one Englishman was worth three Germans' to something from the music hall stage that was no longer believed by the average person. It coincided with demands from America that if Britain wanted help, there should be more genuine war reporting.

Field Marshall Lord Kitchener invited a small party of journalists to the Western Front in January 1916 to observe the situation. Igglesden's inclusion in the party was ostensibly on the orders of Kitchener to write the script for a series of recruiting lectures. He was, after all, honorary recruiting officer for East Kent with the rank of major. In the event, the lectures did not take place because conscription was introduced. However, the visit provided excellent copy for a series of articles in the *Kentish Express*.

A Mere Englishman in America was born when a newly knighted Sir Charles Igglesden was invited to visit the United States as a guest of the Carnegie Peace Institute. He was included in an exclusive party of fourteen British journalists to report back to the UK on how civilised America had become in a few short years since the days of the 'Wild West'. Over three months the journalists, including the editors of *The Times*, the *Daily Express*, *The Scotsman* and the *Belfast Telegraph*, traversed America, west from New York to California and east along the Mexican border to Washington.

Igglesden was distinctly underwhelmed by the new skyscrapers in New York. He called them 'claustrophobic' because they cut out the light and trapped the exhaust fumes, which caused sore throats. However, he was greatly impressed by the way the old Wild West towns such as Denver and Kansas had transformed themselves in under fifty years into beautiful urban townships with wide boulevards and spacious parks.

In Hollywood, he noted that half the actors and directors were British, especially since the advent of the talkies. He met Douglas Fairbanks and his wife, Mary Pickford. Charlie Chaplin, in conversation, revealed himself to be a shrewd businessman.

Igglesden (third from left, front) on his way to America with a party of leading British newspaper editors.

Igglesden with Douglas Fairbanks Senior in Hollywood.

Mary Pickford, with Charles Igglesden (far right).

Igglesden greatly liked New Orleans's old-world feel with buildings to match – some were 200 years old! His favourite city was Washington DC, the presidential city, which was then a dignified place with no skyscrapers. It quite reminded him of home.

His parting thoughts were that greater understanding was needed between the two nations because, after all, they were like father and son who had grown apart because of 3,000 miles of ocean. Education was the answer, so that the two countries might understand one another better.

After Charles's father Henry died in 1907, he seems to have increased his commitment to public service. He was elected to Kent County Council for West Ashford in 1907 and was an Alderman from 1914 until his death in 1949. He was chairman of the Kent Health Committee (today's equivalent of the area's Health Authority) for thirty-five years. Additionally, he was a fellow of the Society of Antiquaries and took a great interest in the Kent Archaeological Society. He served as president of the Association of Men of Kent and Kentish Men, chairman of the Kent County Industrial School and chairman of the Ashford Division of Justices. In Freemasonry, he was a master of the Invicta Lodge and held the rank of Grand Assistant Director of Ceremonies.

Sir Charles Igglesden was a man of unbounded energy and wide-ranging abilities, who was still busy writing his fluent and often scathing editorial comments until shortly before his death in 1949 at the age of 88. His thirty-four volumes of *Saunters Through Kent with Pen and Pencil* will be his lasting testimony.

Many commentators have pigeon-holed Igglesden as a lightweight historian whose books were not in the same scholarly league as Edward Hasted, a century earlier. However, a reviewer in *The Times* acknowledged that they were far more picturesque than Hasted's. Igglesden was a storyteller whose unique anecdotes are part of Kentish lore. And that is what the telling of historical tales has traditionally been.

Here is an example of Igglesden's writing, taken from the first volume, published in 1900, and describing Dungeness:

> Can we be near the bustling world out here at Dungeness? Aye, so close that casting our eyes inland we can plainly distinguish Folkestone, Sandgate, Hythe, Romney and Littlestone on one side, and Rye and Winchelsea on the other, with Lydd further inland. Yet the close proximity of towns does not influence us at Dungeness Point, with its lighthouse – or lighthouses, for there are two Lloyd's signal station not far off – its fishermen's huts dotted

here and there along the beach, the coastguard stations at certain intervals of distance, a couple of lifeboat houses and a few other buildings [...]

On a dreary day the place bears a look of desolation, but on this hot August afternoon everything seems bright. We loll listlessly on the beach; the sun shines overhead from a cloudless sky, while the pebbles at our feet sparkle in its rays; the wavelets lap below us, so innocent-looking, and it seems incredible that ere the moon rises they may be lashing the shore in fury and wreaking destruction around them; big vessels ironclads, ocean greyhounds, graceful sailing craft, yachts and humble tramps pass us around the point, pilot boats skim the surface of rippling waves; fat porpoises roll half-way out of the water, and seagulls dip at the glittering shoals of tiny fish, overhead myriad larks pour forth their song, and plovers scream [...]

Yes, this is Dungeness on a lovely summer's day. What it must be on a winter's night, when the storm clouds burst, the waves go mad, the wind becomes a hurricane, and all the elements combine to wreak their fury upon the devoted ships rolling and tossing about close by ...

There was just one loose end that needed tying up to complete his life's work. Nine villages that appeared as articles in the *Kentish Express* towards the end of his life did not find their way into hardback form. So, a Volume 35 of *Saunters Through Kent* was published posthumously in 2018.

17

The Isle of Sheppey: Cradle of British Aviation, 1909

On 29 November 1913, Britain's First Lord of the Admiralty, Winston S. Churchill, became the world's first government minister to learn to fly. The airfield from which he flew was Eastchurch, on the Isle of Sheppey, the home of Britain's first military flying school, under the auspices of the Royal Naval base at nearby Sheerness.

Winston Churchill learning to fly at Eastchurch.

Muswell Manor, HQ of the Royal Aero Club.

It was only a few years earlier, in 1909, at Shellness, 2½ miles to the east of Eastchurch, that British aviation was born with powered flight. It was at Muswell Manor, Shellness, that the fledgling British Aero Club formed in 1901, and the Short Brothers, the world's first aircraft manufacturers, established themselves.

Next to Muswell Manor was a large field, where the early aviators experimented day after day. Those magnificent men and their crude flying machines included John Moore-Brabazon, Charles S. Rolls (of Rolls-Royce fame), Frank McClean, Ernest Pitman and the Grace brothers, Percy and Frank.

The British Aero Club had first established itself as a hot air balloon club and Short Brothers were balloon manufacturers at Battersea. This all changed in 1909, when they all concentrated their efforts on powered flight and moved to the Isle of Sheppey, where there was more space and they were less likely to attract complaints from docile sheep. The British Aero Club gained the appellation 'Royal' in 1910.

The first aircraft to appear at Shellbeach was Moore-Brabazon's French Voisin, which made its maiden flight of 50 yards on 2 May 1909. This became recognised as the first official powered flight in Britain.

Two days later, the world's first powered aviators, the American Wright Brothers, visited Shellness and granted the Short Brothers the licence to build six Wright Flyers. This was an improved version of the machine in which Orville and Wilbur Wright had achieved their first powered flight at Kittyhawk, North Carolina, in 1903. It is as a result of this deal with the Wright Brothers that Shorts became the world's first aircraft manufacturers.

In 1917, Short Brothers moved from Sheppey to Rochester on the Medway and developed and manufactured their famous Flying Boats and of course the Sterling bomber, which until the Lancaster came along was Britain's frontline

The Royal Aero Club welcomes the Wright brothers to Muswell Manor. Front row: Rolls and Brabazon with the Wright brothers. Back row: the Short brothers.

Wright Flyers, made under licence by Short Brothers.

bomber, for much of the Second World War. After the war, Shorts moved to Belfast, where they are still based and are now part of the Canadian Bombardier Group and Belfast's largest employer. It is interesting to speculate that the Short Brothers would never have got a sniff of the Wright Flyer if the Wright Brothers had not been turned down by not only the American government but also the French, Germans and Japanese.

In 1910, due to the exposed and windy conditions at Shellness, the airfield was moved around the corner to Eastchurch, 2½ miles away, and both Short Brothers and the Royal Aero Club moved to the new site. Among the first pilot's licences granted were to Moore-Brabazon (No. 1), Charles Rolls (No. 2) and Frank McClean.

The memorial to Short Brothers at Shellness.

Frank McClean purchased four Short Brothers planes, which he placed at the disposal of the Royal Naval Base at Sheerness, in order that volunteers from the navy could learn to fly, with the idea that aeroplanes should be used offensively during wartime. However, there was no encouragement from the War Office; indeed, these pioneers had to carry on their crusade amid official neglect, and even ridicule. For it was a fact that in the early days of flying the dangers were considerable, causing occasional deaths. In fact, it was one of the reasons it was not thought wise for Winston Churchill to continue with his flying lessons, because to lose the First Lord of the Admiralty in a flying accident would be 'unfortunate'.

Nevertheless, Churchill was keen to incorporate the new flying machines into the navy's offensive capability, launching the aeroplanes from the decks of specially adapted ships. Remember, this was before the formation of the RAF in 1918. Before then, the army and navy very much went their own way. Eastchurch, therefore, became the research and development base of the Royal Naval Air Service.

During 1909, much progress had been made, aided by the *Daily Mail* and others offering prizes for specific achievements. The *Daily Mail* prize of £1,000 for the first British pilot to make a circular flight of 1 mile using a British aircraft was won by Moore-Brabazon, using a Short No. 2, flying at a height of 20ft.

However, 1910 witnessed both triumph and tragedy. Thomas Sopwith won the prize offered by Baron de Forest to the British pilot who made the furthest non-stop flight into Europe. Climbing to a height of 1,000ft, he covered 177 miles from Eastchurch to Beaumont in Belgium. Sadly, the first tragedy occurred in the summer of 1910, when Charles Rolls became the first of the British pioneer flyers to die in a flying accident, while taking part in a competition at Bournemouth. The second fatality was Cecil Grace, who was competing in the cross-Channel air race that had been won by Sopwith. He became disoriented when he lost his compass and ended up in the North Sea. Neither he nor his machine were ever seen again. A stained-glass memorial window was unveiled to the two aviation pioneers at All Saints Church at Eastchurch by the Archbishop of Canterbury on 27 July 1912.

On a lighter note, Frank McClean caused a national sensation when taking off from the Swale at Harty Ferry in a Short seaplane. He flew through Tower Bridge and under the next six bridges before landing in front of the Houses of Parliament. The police were not amused, although the public were thrilled. However, it did not prevent him from being knighted in the 1926 King's Birthday Honours list for services to aviation.

The crowning glory for Eastchurch and the Isle of Sheppey was the hosting in July 1911 of the International Air Race, sponsored by the rich and sometimes eccentric American publisher James Gordon Bennett. Over 10,000 spectators turned out to see pilots from France, America and Britain complete forty laps round a fixed-circuit course of 94 miles. The winner was an American, Charles Wenman. The previous year's winner was an Englishman, Claude Gilbert White, who could not compete as he was unable to acquire a suitable machine. (Incidentally, the expression 'Gordon Bennett!', denoting incredulous surprise, refers to the outrageous behaviour of James Gordon Bennett Jr.)

During the First World War the Royal Aero Club buildings and flying ground were offered to the Royal Navy Air Services (RNAS). The airfield was becoming home to several training and research facilities and at the end of 1916, a gunnery school also came into being.

In April 1917, Horace Short died at his home at Parsonage Farm, Eastchurch, following which Short Brothers ended its association with Eastchurch. Its buildings were taken over by the Royal Naval Air Service.

On 25 December 1918, the Air Ministry purchased the Eastchurch flying ground and it became a specialist training facility for armourers, but when the Second World War broke out Eastchurch, because of its location, was considered too vulnerable to enemy attack, so the Armament School was relocated to Pembury, near Tonbridge, and Cosford in Shropshire.

After being used as a reception and training centre for Polish airmen, who had escaped to England, it was again considered too vulnerable to enemy attack, so the Poles were moved to Blackpool. Eastchurch was badly bombed and proved to be of little use as an offensive airfield until the latter part of the war, when rocket-firing courses for Hawker Typhoon squadrons were organised. Also, with the war turning in favour of the Allies, it was felt safe to bring up Spitfire and Hurricane squadrons to Eastchurch as part of an exercise called Spartan. Crews operated from tented accommodation to replicate conditions that would be found in a big push through Europe.

The war ended on 8 May 1945 when the Germans surrendered. Eastchurch aerodrome was formally closed on 30 August 1946. Despite several abortive attempts to use the airfield complex for housing, the Home Office in 1949 requisitioned the whole site as an open prison. All traces of the early pioneers were effectively wiped out except Muswell Manor, so a permanent memorial was erected at the crossroads in the centre of Eastchurch village. It was officially unveiled on 25 July 1955 in the presence of John T.C. Moore-Brabazon

(Lord Brabazon) and others involved in the early days of flight in Sheppey. Sad to say, this was all quickly forgotten in the prosaic setting that is now Eastchurch Open Prison.

Somehow, the Isle of Sheppey covered in sheep and an Open Prison doesn't quite have the romance one might associate with the birthplace of British aviation. There is a recently extended museum on the prison site, which is open to the public, but much more needs to be done in terms of recreating the early flying experience. There are some 1912 hangers which currently belong to the prison. In the words of English Heritage, they are 'the most valuable aviation architecture left in Europe' and 'they're currently standing empty'. If the museum can take them over, they might soon be able to show off some early aircraft used by those very first pioneers. The expanding museum deserves every success. After all, aviation is one of the greatest inventions of the twentieth century and the crucial role played by the Isle of Sheppey needs greater recognition. It remains truly one of Kent's finest historical jewels.

The Aviation Museum at Eastchurch, Isle of Sheppey, was extended in February 2024.

18

Chitty Chitty Bang Bang and Count Zborowski, 1920

A much-loved children's book and adapted for the stage and screen, *Chitty Chitty Bang Bang* has as its inspiration two unlikely sources: James Bond and a famous and flamboyant motor-racing driver, Count Louis Zborowski.

The James Bond connection is 007's author, Ian Fleming, who, as a young man in the early 1930s, was engaged in the family business of merchant banking. He was a frequent visitor to Higham Park on the outskirts of Bridge, a village 3 miles south of Canterbury. It was the home of merchant banker Walter Whigham, a partner in the firm Robert Fleming, which had been founded by Ian Fleming's grandfather. However, the point of particular interest is that Higham Park had been owned by the aforementioned Count Louis Zborowski until his death in a racing accident in 1924.

It was on one of Ian Fleming's visits to Higham Park, long before he wrote his first James Bond novel, late one evening over a glass of port or two, that Walter Whigham related a most remarkable tale about Count Louis Zborowski, which was to be the inspiration for a children's novel. It wasn't written until over thirty years later, in 1961, shortly after he had finished his ninth James Bond novel.

As related by Walter Whigham, the Zborowski story begins in late-nineteenth-century New York, with Louis Zborowski's father, Count Elliot Zborowski, an American of Polish extraction. The title 'count' is of doubtful provenance, being more of a family legend, and Elliot's father Martin never adopted the title. But Elliot, bowing to his grandfather's wish, adopted the title after his father's death, and in time, it became accepted in the highest social circles.

Count Zborowski's family were extremely wealthy, owning much property in New York including land around Central Park. Elliot was a bit of a playboy, who had a penchant for horse riding, at which he was extremely accomplished. He also had an eye for the ladies.

He had heard much about the fox-hunting scene in England, so in 1885, armed with his title and money, he visited Melton Mowbray in Leicestershire, home to the famous Quorn, the oldest hunt in England, dating back to 1686. He soon became an accepted part of the hunting fraternity, not only became of his obvious aristocratic credentials but also because he was a particularly accomplished horse rider. As a result, in 1886 he purchased a fine mansion called Coventry House in Melton Mowbray.

It wasn't long before all the great and the good were making a beeline to Coventry House, including the Prince of Wales. Needless to say, the count was made to feel quite at home in England.

Because all his business interests were in New York, he travelled backwards and forwards between America and England and it was during a visit to New York in 1890 that he met an unhappily married Margaret de Stuers (*née* Margaret Laura Astor Carey), who was a granddaughter of William Astor, reputed at the time to be America's wealthiest man. So Margaret had inherited wealth in her own right.

Elliot and Margaret fell in love, which in 1892 resulted in her somewhat messy divorce. Margaret and Elliot married later that year, but their New England friends treated them as social outcasts, so they decamped to England, where they were accepted without demur. This was partly due to the fact that the English aristocracy, to shore up their bankrupt estates, sought American heiresses to marry and therefore an American woman on the social scene was not uncommon. No doubt Margaret, being an Astor, soon made friends.

To complete their membership of high society, they bought a grand house in London for the summer social season to complement Coventry House in the countryside of Leicestershire; they truly had arrived, aristocracy imported, lock, stock and barrel from America. Elliot also became a naturalised British subject.

They lived mainly at Coventry House and not long after they had settled in, Elliot became interested in the new mode of transport, motor cars and particularly motor racing. In fact, it became an obsession and it wasn't long before his stable was closed, horses sold and racing cars appeared in their place.

In 1895, their son Louis was born and their life seemed complete. But in 1903, tragedy struck, when Elliot was killed in a motor-racing accident in Nice. Not long after Elliot's death, his widow Margaret, together with her 8-year-old son, moved to Bridge Hill House on the outskirts of the village of Bridge, 3 miles south of Canterbury. It is not clear why Margaret chose to move to Bridge.

When he was of age, Louis was sent to Eton, like all of his aristocratic peers, but he abhorred life in what was a traditional English public school. He did not apply himself to his studies and hated the cruel regime. So it was no surprise when he was sent down.

Bridge Hill House was reasonably substantial but Margaret had her eye on an even more substantial dwelling, Higham Park, up on Barham Downs. Bridge Hill House (now a Grade II-listed building converted into apartments), although prestigious, had a slightly tarnished reputation, having been the headquarters of the Canterbury Races, which took place for 200 years until 1868 up on Barham Downs. Bridge Hill House was, as a result, popularly known as the Horse and Groom, which was hardly in keeping with Margaret's aristocratic pedigree and huge wealth.

Higham, on the other hand, was originally built in the reign of Elizabeth I and rebuilt in 1768, and contained forty bedrooms, a ballroom and a cocktail lounge. It was ideal. It did, however, require much refurbishment. Throughout its long history, it had been visited by the rich and famous: Mozart, Jane Austen and Charles de Gaulle, to name just a few. So Margaret was undeterred by its dilapidated state and purchased Higham Park for £17,500 and spent a further £50,000 on completely renovating the house and giving it a Palladian façade. Sadly, she died in 1911 from a bout of influenza, just before the renovations were completed.

Baroness Zborowski left her entire estate to her only child, 16-year-old Louis. The estate in question consisted of £11 million in cash and real estate in Manhattan, New York, and several blocks on Fifth Avenue. He was reckoned to be one of the four richest under-21-year-olds in the world.

It was at this point, free from academic expectations, that he was able to give bent to his true forte, engineering, and like his father, a desire to become a motor-racing driver. He set up a large workshop on the Higham estate and

Higham, the home of Count Zborowski.

Count Zborowski at Brooklands.

employed engineers and mechanics to enable to him not only to assemble a fleet of racing cars but also to design his own extra powerful racing cars.

The fleet of cars consisted of Bugattis, Mercedes Benz and Salmsons. His own designs consisted of the immortal, huge aero-engined monsters, the 23-litre 'Chitty Bang Bangs' – so called because of the noise they made when starting up.

The young Count Louis raced his monster at Brooklands, winning one race at an average speed of 100.75mph. Three versions of this car were produced. A later design, the Higham Special, broke the world land speed record at 171.02mph with J.G. Parry Thomas at the wheel.

While continuing to race, Count Louis extended his interest into other forms of locomotion, building a 15in-gauge railway in the grounds of Higham. More importantly, with Captain John Howey, he built the Romney Hythe & Dymchurch Railway, which today is one of Kent's greatest tourist attractions. Count Louis also had an aeroplane at nearby Bekesbourne Airfield and a motor yacht at Faversham.

All the while he still pursued his great passion, racing for Aston Martin and Mercedes Benz, whom he had supported financially. It was while driving the latter in the Italian Grand Prix in 1924 that he hit a tree and died instantly. He was just 29 years old.

Ian Fleming remembered seeing Count Louis racing at Brooklands as a child. This story stayed firmly lodged in the back of Fleming's mind for another thirty years, long after he had forsaken the world of merchant banking and taken up the pen and written nine of his thirteen James Bond novels.

In fact, it was in 1961, when he was convalescing from a serious heart attack at his seaside home in St Margaret's Bay near Dover, that he wrote *Chitty Chitty Bang Bang*. His doctor had forbidden him to do any serious writing, but he considered that writing a children's book was not really serious writing. Sadly, he had a second and fatal heart attack three years later, in 1964. He was only 58.

Count Louis Zborowski has been immortalised in the *Chitty Chitty Bang Bang* book and there are also statues of him at Brooklands and Le Mans. One of the Chitty Bang Bang cars can be viewed at the National Motor Museum at Beaulieu. In 1968, Fleming's book was adapted by United Artists into a highly successful motion picture by Roald Dahl, starring Dick Van Dyke, Sally Ann Howes and Max Wall. The story was then adapted into a stage musical, with music and lyrics by Richard and Robert Sherman. The show premiered at the London Palladium in 2002, before opening again on Broadway in 2005.

19

H.E. Bates and *The Darling Buds of May*, 1930

It would be a reasonable supposition that the author of *The Darling Buds of May*, that quintessential portrait of Kentish village life in the 1950s, was a man of Kent. Not so. H.E. (Herbert Ernest) Bates was born and spent the first twenty-five years of his life in Rushden, Northamptonshire. However, his love affair with the county began in 1926 when, at the age of 20, he was discovered as a writing talent by the legendary Edward Garnett, then the reader at Jonathan Cape publishers. After an initial meeting in London, Bates was invited down to Garnett's home, The Cearne, at Crockham Hill near Westerham, to discuss his literary aspirations further. He was absolutely captivated by the house's location on the greensand ridge overlooking the seemingly infinite expanse of the Weald of Kent.

The Cearne had been designed in medieval style for Garnett and his wife, Constance, by a disciple of William Morris. Constance, like her husband, was a literary icon, famous for her translation of many of the Russian classics, including those by Turgenev, which the young Bates knew well. It was Constance who created The Cearne's celebrated garden, which was noted for its rockery and flower garden despite being set on intractable sandstone. This also made a great impression on Bates because he had inherited a passion for flowers from his father and maternal grandmother.

As a result of this initial visit, he determined that one day he would not only make his home in Kent but would create a garden in similar fashion to that of Constance Garnett. During the next five years, Bates established himself as a writer of great promise, travelling frequently to London and The Cearne to see his literary mentor, Edward, and his gardening guru, Constance. On occasions, he was accompanied by his childhood sweetheart, Madge, and she too fell in love with Kent. In August 1930, they tramped over a good part of the county looking for possible houses in which to live.

They came across Pluckley, which stands on the same greensand ridge as The Cearne, but 20 miles to the west. Toiling up the ridge to Pluckley, they came to the village of Little Chart and knew immediately that this was where they would settle. They were enchanted by the village cottages and its impressive pub, the Swan Inn, all with their ubiquitous Dering windows (you will perhaps remember those from Chapter 10). Opposite the pub is the eighteenth-century Ford Paper Mill with its two picturesque feeder lakes alongside the River Stour, where H.E. Bates was to spend many happy hours fishing.

Less than a mile to the east lay what was reputedly the oldest hop garden in England, next to a neo-Catholic church whose sponsors for centuries had been the Darrell family, who occupied Calehill House to the north. Sadly, this was demolished in 1951 and the church was reduced to a ruin by one of Hitler's doodlebugs in 1945, an event witnessed by the Bates family. All that remains today is the tower, protected by English Heritage (a replacement church was built in 1956 opposite the pub). Another attraction was the fledgling River Stour which encircles Little Chart on its journey to Ashford and thence forward to Canterbury before disgorging into the sea at Thanet.

By an amazing coincidence, one of the Bateses' friends from the London literary scene lived at Rooting Manor, on the outskirts of Little Chart. Violet Dean was the sister of film producer Basil Dean and part of the Longman family of book publishers. She was keen to help the young couple in their house-hunting so invited them down to her home for a weekend in February 1931. During their stay, they discovered a disused granary in Little Chart Forstal, which had planning permission for conversion into a house. By scrimping and scraping and securing a loan from the bank, they raised the necessary £600 to acquire the granary and pay for its conversion into a four-bedroomed home.

Today, Little Chart Forstal has an idyllic setting around a village green, together with a cricket pitch, and surrounded by a dozen houses of stone, half-timbered and soft, bronzy-red brick. In 1931 it was more rustic, showing clear evidence that, as a forstal, it was where, in former times, cattle were assembled in front of the farmhouse on the way to Ashford Market. In July of that year, the newly wed Mr and Mrs Bates moved into The Granary and the real work

H.E. Bates's local, The Swan at Little Chart.

Remains of the original Little Chart Church destroyed by one of Hitler's doodlebugs in 1944.

Little Chart Church before it was reduced to ruins by a doodlebug.

Little Chart Forstal as viewed from The Granary.

started to convert a disused farmyard and an acre of land infested with giant dock and thistle into a garden to match that of The Cearne. H.E. Bates virtually gave up writing that summer to lay the foundations for the wonderful garden he duly created. Violet Dean assisted once again. She had a disused quarry on the Rooting Manor estate, and she allowed Bates to take away great cheese-green lumps of Kentish ragstone for his rock garden.

H.E. Bates spent the rest of his life at Little Chart Forstal raising his four children, working on the celebrated garden and describing in his later novels the joys of the Kentish countryside. He was particularly fond of the little stone bridge which spanned the fledgling River Stour over Ram Lane, close to The Granary. The family would picnic in the meadow below the bridge while observing the passing of trout and kingfishers.

In his book *Through the Woods*, published in 1936, he describes in detail the effect of the changing seasons on Coldhams Woods, not far from The Granary. The path through this small wood runs down to a small wooden bridge over the Stour, producing a felicitous combination of light and shade, with the river no more than a brook at this point, 'jingling and diddling and rippling over a bed of sand and stone with water as clear as wine'. It is here, in this wood, that he would often encounter the dreaded gamekeepers with their dogs and guns, who he freely admits to hating because of their double-dealing life of having to preserve to kill and kill to preserve. Above all, he resented their unpleasant attitude not just to poachers, who were legitimate targets, but to all country-lovers who dared to veer from the designated footpaths to admire the flora and fauna.

In the second volume of his autobiography, *The Blossoming World*, he describes the almost surreal experience in the fateful summer of 1940, observing the Battle of Britain taking place almost exclusively in the Kentish skies above him. He was later to incorporate this experience into his novel *A Moment in Time*. Shortly after this experience, Bates was commissioned into the RAF to become its writer in residence (a unique appointment for the armed forces), publishing his short stories under the pseudonym 'Flying Officer X'.

An interesting observation he makes in his autobiography is that this part of Kent was particularly healthy because it was rich in iodine, because Kent is practically an island, with two-thirds of its boundaries being water. He also describes what he calls the 'English vendange', the hop-picking season, which he likens to a festival when Cockneys from London joined the people of Kent in a sort of pagan rite. It is sadly no more as they now pull the vines by machine.

The Granary, H.E. Bates's home for forty years.

The garden created by H.E. Bates at The Granary.

The Darling Buds of May series of novels, featuring Pa Larkin and his family, was made into a very successful television series in the early 1990s, starring David Jason, Pam Ferris and a young actress by the name of Catherine Zeta-Jones. It was largely filmed in and around Pluckley and Little Chart.

H.E. Bates sadly died prematurely in 1974 but his garden lives on and his literary legacy runs to more than forty novels and collections of short stories, many featuring his beloved Kent.

The bridge over the River Stour in Coldham Wood near H.E. Bates's home.

20

The Tithe Rebellion, 1935

In 1937, in a field beside the A20, 3½ miles to the west of Ashford, a monument was erected to the memory of the Reverend Roderick Kedward by grateful tithe-payers. The field was in a corner of Beechbrook Farm, on the outskirts of the village of Westwell, where Kedward was born and where the family had farmed since 1870. In 1998, the monument was removed to Ashford New Market. It is inscribed as follows:

> In memory of Roderick Morris Kedward, President of the National Tithe Payers Association 1931–37, MP for Ashford 1929–31. Born 1881. Died 1937. This stone is a token of gratitude for the splendid service he rendered in the tithe payers' cause and of admiration of his character. This site forms part of his Farm where he was born and where he suffered repeated distraints of tithe.

The Reverend Roderick Kedward was one of the leading figures in the so-called Tithe War, between 1918–39, which was a revolt by almost 100,000 tithe-paying farmers and landowners in England, against the iniquitous 3,500-year-old tithe, first mentioned in the Bible's Old Testament (Leviticus 27:30).

The tithe was a form of taxation whereby farmers had to donate 10 per cent of their crops, cattle and hops to the local church to support the clergy. This gave rise to the erection of Tithe Barns usually adjacent to the church, where the farm produce was stored. This ancient practice led to disputes and uncertainty due to the vagaries of the weather affecting crop yields and thus the amount of tithe payable. So, in 1836, the variable tithe was replaced by what was effectively a tithe tax of fixed amount. Even if the harvest was poor

The tithe protest at Beechbrook Farm.

the farmer had to pay the fixed rent tithe. This caused great hardship to the farmers, particularly during an agricultural depression, which at this time had gripped England.

It wasn't only farmers who had to pay this tithe rent charge but landowners who had acquired what were farmlands at the time of Henry VIII's Reformation, where he diverted the lands of the Catholic monasteries, not only to his newly founded Church of England, but to lay freeholders who were supporters of the monarch. The universities of Oxford and Cambridge, whose colleges had monastic origins, were allowed to keep their considerable landholdings tithe-free. A natural consequence of the fixed tithe was to make the Church of England extremely unpopular with local farming communities, particularly the Archbishop of Canterbury Cosmo Lang, whose effigy was often burnt at the frequent demonstrations against the tithe.

Although it affected lands across England, it was in East Anglia and Kent that the leaders of the tithe-payers' revolt arose: A.G. Mobbs, a farmer in East Anglia, and Reverend Roderick Kedward, whose family had farmed in Kent since 1870.

Beechbrook Farm today.

The Wesleyan chapel in Hothfield where Kedward taught at Sunday school, now a domestic dwelling.

Roderick Morris Kedward was born at Beechbrook Farm, Westwell, in Kent, on 14 September 1881, one of fourteen children of William Wesley Kedward and Eliza (née Morris). The Kedwards were firm Methodists and Liberals and four of their sons were to become Wesleyan ministers. The family worshipped at the tiny Hothfield Chapel, next to the Westwell Workhouse where, as a young man, Roderick Kedward taught at the Sunday school and became a local preacher, before spending time at the Mission Home in Rochdale, which was the headquarters of the Methodist evangelist movement. He soon became a travelling evangelist and famously spent time in Worcester Gaol for illegally preaching on a local village green. After protests by the local Methodists, he was released on the orders of the Home Office.

He became a minister in 1903, after training at Richmond College, and served at Lydd on Romney Marsh for four years, while continuing to tour the country recruiting converts to Methodism. His next appointment was in Hull, where he served three Wesleyan congregations in the slum area of Sculcoates. It was there that he gained the title of 'The Fighting Parson' after beating off a drunken, wife-battering docker. His great and lasting achievement in Hull was raising the funds for building the Methodist Central Hall, which was opened in October 1910 with a weekly congregation of 2,000. During this time, he married Daisy Annie Frederick in 1906. They had three sons and three daughters.

He became a popular figure in Hull and soon after the outbreak of the First World War in 1914, the soldiers of the East Yorkshire Regiment petitioned the War Office for Kedward to be appointed Chaplain of one of the Hull Battalions. He served in Egypt before the division was transferred to the Western Front. Kedward was one of the horrendous casualties of the Battle of the Somme. He was invalided out of the army in October 1916.

After recovering his health, he took up the post of minister at the South London Methodist Mission based at Bermondsey Central Hall. He became a member of Bermondsey Borough Council from 1920–25 in what was one of the poorest and most deprived boroughs in London. The main source of employment was Surrey Docks. He successfully stood for Parliament in Bermondsey West in 1923 as the Liberal candidate, but was defeated in 1924 when the Liberal–Conservative pact collapsed and the first Labour government came to power.

Kedward had been appointed Superintendent of the South London Mission in 1918 and was to spend the rest of his life working in Bermondsey. However, he had continued living in Westwell and had moved with his family to Pine

Trees, a stone's throw from the Hothfield Chapel, while continuing to help run the family farm at Beechbrook, which was now tenanted by his brother-in-law, Mr A.T. Chapman. He witnessed at first hand the distraints against farm property and livestock by County Court Baliffs on behalf of tithe owners.

He now became actively involved in fighting the tithe-payers' cause and soon realised that to effect a change in the law he needed to return to Parliament. This he did in May 1929, when he was elected Liberal MP for Ashford, ending a forty-four-year domination of the seat by the Conservative Party. He immediately introduced the Tithe Remission Bill under the ten-minute rule. However, the bill made no progress as the Labour government was defeated in the ensuing election in 1931 and Kedward lost his seat to the Honourable Michael Knatchbull, the Conservative candidate.

Kedward became President of the National Tithepayers' Association in 1931 and led demonstrations all over East Anglia and Kent. His brother-in-law was distrained against many times on behalf of the landowner, Merton College Oxford.

In April 1935, tithe-payers' anger overflowed in Kent. The immediate cause was an auction at Beechbrook Farm in Westwell of nine cows seized from Mr A.T. Chapman, the Reverend Kedward's brother-in-law. An effigy of Archbishop Cosmo Lang was burnt, demonstrators blew whistles and trumpets and fireworks were thrown into the auction ring. Wives and daughters of protesters lay down in front of lorries loaded with oats seized from the farm. The protestors' actions were successful, and the auction was abandoned. The press had a field day and questions were asked in the House of Commons.

During the years 1931–35, the tithe-payers' mood generally was one of angry defiance against the Church of England, such as had not been witnessed in rural England for a very long time. The press could hardly contain itself as it ran anti-Church headlines and splashed sensational pictures of rural England in chaos and open revolt. In 1936, following a royal commission, a new Tithe Act converted the tithe into an annuity redemption payment which was integrated into the tax system and would phase out the tithe altogether over sixty years.

Reverend Kedward died the following year on 3 March 1937, following a sudden illness (a duodenal ulcer). The tithe movement subsided soon after, but Kedward had effectively finished off the iniquitous tithe, and after forty years, in 1977, tithe annuities ceased, much to the relief of all concerned, particularly the Church, whose image had been badly damaged.

The memorial to Roderick Kedward at Ashford New Market.

21

The Romanovs in Kent, 1949

Not many parish churches in Kent, or indeed England, have the earthly remains of a royal prince buried in their churchyard. But St Mary's Church, Norton, near Faversham, can make that proud claim, for it plays host to the grave of Prince Andrei Alexandrovich (1897–1981) of the Russian Imperial House of Romanov, which had ruled Russia since 1612 and which includes among its members Peter the Great and Catherine the Great.

Born in the Winter Palace, St Petersburg, in 1897, Prince Andrew was a grandson of Tsar Alexander III and the eldest nephew of Alexander's son, Nicholas II, the last Tsar of Russia. Along with his family, Nicholas II was murdered by the Bolsheviks in 1918.

In December 1918, Prince Andrew avoided the same fate as his uncle by travelling from the family estate in Crimea with his wife Elsa and father Sandro (Grand Duke Alexander Mikhailovich) on HMS *Forsyth*, which George V of the United Kingdom had sent to take Sandro to the Paris Peace Conference in a fruitless attempt to gain support for the White Russian Army. (Sandro had been a very important military figure in pre-revolutionary Russia, having founded the Russian Air Force as well as being Admiral of the Russian Fleet.)

Four months later, the rest of the family, including Sandro's wife Xenia and her mother, Empress Dagmar, escaped aboard HMS *Marlborough* and were taken to London. George V and Tsar Nicholas II were cousins because their mothers were sisters and princesses of the Danish royal family, and they were very close on a personal level. However, most of the grand dukes and their families were murdered by the Bolsheviks, thus eliminating the direct descendants of the Tsars.

St Mary's Church, Norton.

Prince Andrei Alexandrovich.

After two years in France, mainly on the Riviera, during which time Andrew and Elsa's first two children were born, they moved to England to join Andrew's mother Xenia, who had been granted a grace-and favour-house by George V – Frogmore, near Windsor – where they resided for nearly twenty years. Their third child, Prince Andrew, was born there in 1923.

In 1939 they were granted another grace-and-favour house, Wilderness House near Hampton Court, where tragically Elsa died after a German bombing raid in 1940. She was only 51 and had been suffering from cancer for some time. To escape the Blitz, the family moved up to Balmoral in Scotland.

It was while living on the Balmoral Estate that Prince Andrew renewed his acquaintance with Nadene McDougall, from the flour-milling family. They had met in London before the war. They fell in love and married in 1942.

They were married in Norton Parish Church because Nadine's mother, Sylvia, and father, Herbert McDougall, had lived in the area since they eloped there to get married in 1906, when they moved into Provender House in Norton, which Sylvia's mother Constance had rented from the Knatchbull family in 1890. After Constance's death in 1912, Sylvia and Herbert McDougall purchased Provender House.

After the Anglican service in St Mary's, Norton, conducted by the Archbishop of Canterbury, they dashed off to St James's Church, Sheldwich, to have a Russian Orthodox Ceremony, permission for which was given by the Archbishop. The reception was held at Lees Court, Sheldwich, the home of Sylvia's sister Pamela, Countess Sondes.

After their marriage, Prince Andrew and Nadine rented Lynsted Court because the army had requisitioned Provender House, where it was intended that they should live with Nadine's mother Sylvia. They eventually moved into Provender in 1949 just before the birth of their daughter, Princess Olga, in 1950.

Provender House is a sprawling thirteenth-century mansion set among the fields and cherry orchards in a typically idyllic Kentish landscape, with the church only 600m to the west across the fields. It occupies a site of 35½ acres and is a kaleidoscope of historic architecture, from the thirteenth-century core, with additions from the fourteenth (the magnificent Crown Post room), fifteenth, seventeenth and eighteenth centuries.

Prince Andrew lived at Provender for thirty-two years and assumed the life of a country squire, living quietly and almost reclusively with his glamorous wife Nadine, who was an extrovert and generally made the speeches when they were guests of honour at local events.

Provender House in the process of restoration by Princess Olga.

Princess Olga pointing out the magnificent Crown Post.

It was a far cry from the Winter Palace in St Petersburg, where Andrew was born and grew up. He was looked after in his infancy by an English nanny and educated by private tutors. When he was older, as eldest nephew, he was taken on manoeuvres by the Tsar, and when the First World War broke out he was in the elite Chevalier Guards. He met Rasputin on many occasions and thought him not a bad person.

Prince Andrew was an extremely talented painter and wood carver. He painted not only landscapes and portraits but also extremely funny caricatures, which he would compose on social occasions under the table, so to speak, while observing those around him. As well as selling his paintings, he even engaged his talents in a business, selling designer handbags and costume jewellery using lapis lazuli until he was defrauded by his business partner.

Andrew and Nadine regularly went to London to the Dorchester and Claridge's and were members of several clubs, including the Edmundo Ros and the Lansdowne, where they indulged their passion for dancing. He was a very accomplished and flamboyant dancer, as his daughter Princess Olga recalls somewhat enviously.

However, he was happiest when pottering around the garden dressed in shabby old clothes and was often mistaken for the gardener! He had green fingers and was brilliant at growing things. He was a great stamp collector and was very knowledgeable and always got the *Stanley Gibbons Catalogue*.

In her recently published autobiography, *A Wild and Barefoot Romanov*, Princess Olga recalls her father happily pushing her around the adjoining farm in her pram before going home to cook the lunch or dinner. Cooking was a skill he learned from the French chefs at the Winter Palace. Although Olga had a nanny, her father often used to bathe her. She also recalls that they had two Christmas celebrations, one on 25 December and then a Russian one on 7 January. However, interestingly, Olga never learned Russian.

Although her father was a relatively old parent (aged 54 when she was born), Olga recalls that he was very active, taking her for walks in the woods where he would build little houses for her out of twigs and sticks and would make a whole little village. He also carved all the furniture for her dolls house. He was a very hands-on parent.

When Prince Andrew died in 1981, the Parish Church of St Mary's, Norton, was temporarily turned into a Russian Orthodox Church for the occasion and he was buried in the graveyard at St Mary's, where in 2000, his wife Nadine was buried alongside him. Prince Andrew's legacy lives on through his daughter, Princess Olga and her three nephews, children of her half-brother, Andrew, who died a few years ago at his home in California aged 94.

Princess Olga lives at Provender and has, with the help of English Heritage, spent a small fortune on restoring it to its former glory, mainly by selling the 'family silver' and turning the house into a business that is open to the public for twenty-eight days of the year with tours conducted by Princess Olga herself. Parties of up to fifty-five are catered for, including a sumptuous afternoon tea.

The restoration work goes on and has been an all-consuming passion for Princess Olga, who is desperate to preserve a unique building and keep the Romanov connection alive. The historian Charles Igglesden described the name Provender as 'euphonious', and the same can be said for its most illustrious owners, the Kentish Romanovs, who have incidentally spelt the name as Romanoff since the Revolution.

22

Decline and Fall of a Flawed Genius in the Forgotten Art of Printing, 1950

On 28 April 1980, a celebration was held at Stationers' Hall in the City of London to commemorate the thirtieth birthday of Westerham Press. A piece of music, 'Fanfares and Dances', was commissioned from the composer Charles Barnes and performed in the gallery of hall by the BBC Welsh Brass Ensemble and broadcast by the BBC.

Westerham Press, with its enigmatic founder, Rowley Atterbury, had in three decades established itself as, arguably, Europe's finest colour printer. In 1965, it became the first company in Europe to introduce computer-assisted typesetting. Westerham Press was responsible for the most significant changes in printing technology since the days of William Caxton, 500 years before.

It is hard to comprehend that the small town of Westerham, 10 miles west of Sevenoaks, in the heart of the Darenth Valley, was the 1960s equivalent of California's Silicon Valley. The area does have form: William Caxton, the father of British printing, was born not far away, in the Weald – possibly Tenterden or Hadlow – in 1450.

However, within four years of the Stationers' Hall celebration, Westerham Press was blown away by the harsh realities of 1980s monetarism, the 'greedy' print unions and, it must be said, poor management. How did this happen?

Rowley Atterbury was undoubtedly a genius and a man of great personal charm. He was a salesman extraordinaire and had the ability to think the unthinkable. His mind knew no conventional boundaries because at heart he was a rebel – just like his ancestor, the Jacobite Dr Francis Atterbury, Dean of Westminster and Bishop of Rochester, who in 1722 was confined in the Tower of London for his anti-Establishment writings and orations.

Rowley Streatfeild Atterbury was born in 1920, the son of a career diplomat who was in the service of the Sudan government. His mother, Barbara, was the sister of the children's writer Noel Streatfeild, who was to play an important part in Rowley's life. Rowley attended Colchester Royal Grammar School, Essex, as a boarder and was extremely unhappy and achieved very little academically.

On the advice of a family friend, he joined the RAF as a boy entrant in 1937 to finish his education and be trained in a career. In the eight years until the end of the Second World War, he wrote training manuals in relation to bombs and guns. When he left the RAF in 1945, he used his writing experience to obtain work with the publishers Faber & Faber. This was to be the springboard that projected this late developer on his true path.

At Faber & Faber, he worked alongside the great typographer Berthold Wolpe on designing the books. Wolpe, who was responsible for many of Faber & Faber's striking book covers, sent Rowley to the Central School of Art and Design in the Bloomsbury area of London, to improve his knowledge, and shortly afterwards, he got him a part-time job at the Camberwell School of Art in south-east London, teaching graphic art. After five years at Faber & Faber improving his book design and production skills, Rowley concluded that publishing was not for him. He decided, instead, to set up as a printer.

The garage at Buckham Thorns where Westerham Press began.

In 1942, Rowley had married Audrey Holman (who was later famous as the puppeteer for the BBC *Watch with Mother* programmes) and he had a son, Paul (today seen regularly as a ceramics expert on BBC's *Antiques Roadshow*). In 1947, his mother's family, the Streatfeilds, presented him with an opportunity to share a rather grand house in Westerham with an aged aunt. It was called Buckham Thorns and, importantly, it had a large garage that in 1950 would prove ideal to house a small printing unit. And so, the Westerham Press was launched.

Rowley's mother-in-law lent him £200 to buy his first printing equipment second-hand. It had been used by the Polish government in exile in London during the Second World War to produce propaganda from a basement flat in Clerkenwell, central London. It comprised a treadle-operated Harrild Bremner platen and a guillotine, plus an assortment of type and accessories.

The arrival of this printing works into the garage of Buckham Thorns so enraged the senior members of the Streatfeild family that Rowley was asked to leave. 'Going into trade' was considered beyond the pale. Fortunately, Rowley found a large, empty home, Prospect House, in Westerham High Street, and in a nearby field discovered a large outbuilding called Wellers Shed. They became the headquarters and works of the fledgling Westerham Press for the next ten years.

Rowley's ambition was to emulate the high standards set by the London-based print companies Curwen Press and Shenval Press in the field of colour printing and to this end, he acquired, in 1952, a Heidelberg cylinder press. Thus began the pursuit of excellence that was to become Westerham's watchword. He not only established an enviable reputation as a printer, but also as a typographer and designer.

In its early days, Westerham Press was financed by a group of supporters and investors, who included Joyce Boosey (of the music publishers Boosey & Hawkes), Berthold Wolpe and three of the company's early employees, Herbert Bowles, Len Turley and Bernard Bart. Westerham's first book printed on the Heidelberg cylinder machine was for George Rainbird, of Rainbird McLean. The high standards achieved with this book led to a lifelong association with Rainbird and his book-publishing empire and in turn led to work for the Folio Society, Penguin Books, the British Council and the Marley Tile Company.

By the end of the 1950s Westerham Press was firmly established with its own monotype Heidelberg platen and vertical Miehle. It also bought Stratton House in Westerham High Street, which housed the accounts department and the planning department.

Westerham Press staff picture in 1959 with Rowley at far right.

All was going well with Westerham Press, but not the Atterbury marriage. Audrey Atterbury was in great demand by the BBC for such programmes as *Andy Pandy* (based, it is said, on their son Paul), *The Flower Pot Men* and *The Woodentops*. This meant that Audrey could no longer help Rowley with Westerham's business. She spent many nights away from home at the BBC, which put a strain on the marriage. In 1956 Audrey left her husband and went to live in Highgate. They soon divorced and the next year Rowley married Mary Harman, a key employee running the accounts department at Westerham. They had a son, Francis.

In 1957 Rowley installed a filmsetter and was keen to experiment with other new technologies. Having concluded that the future lay in the lithographic printing process and not the 'hot metal' letterpress system, he decided in 1959 to set up an experimental factory at Biggin Hill in a disused sergeants' mess, exclusively using the litho-printing process. In 1958, a visit to the Paris Printing Exhibition prompted the ordering of a prototype four-colour Kolibri litho-printing machine, followed in 1960 by the four-colour Nebiolo; the first in the UK.

It was at this point that Max Rayne, a property developer and philanthropist – later Lord Rayne – appeared on the scene to play a pivotal role as the catalyst for Westerham's great leap into the brave new world of computer typesetting. Rowley had met Rayne in 1955 when Rayne's company, London Merchant Securities, was in the process of bidding to develop the precincts of St Paul's Cathedral. He needed, in a hurry, a high-quality promotional booklet to support his bid. The designer and artist Charles Mozley had designed the booklet and recommended Westerham Press as printers.

Rowley Atterbury and Lord Rayne.

Rayne was greatly impressed with the finished article and was even more impressed with Westerham's charismatic young owner. As a result, his company, London Merchant Securities (LMS), took a 10 per cent shareholding in Westerham Press. Then, in 1960, LMS rescued the debt-ridden printing giant Hazell-Sun (later to become the British Printing Corporation, acquired by the infamous Robert Maxwell, but that's another story altogether). As a result, LMS became a major shareholder in Hazell-Sun and now found itself with an interest in two printing companies.

According to Rowley's autobiography, in early 1963, in the company of Rowley and Hazell-Sun's Geoffrey Crowther, Rayne posed the question, 'What will be the next major new development in printing technology?' Without hesitation, Rowley replied, 'The application of data processing to [computer] typesetting.' Rayne responded by telling them to get on with it and form a company dedicated to computer typesetting.

Some research had already been undertaken in the USA by a company called Rocappi (Research on Computer Applications to Printing and Publishing Industries). Westerham's technical expert, Duncan MacIntyre, went to the USA and came back with favourable reports of both Rocappi and its Yorkshire-born technical expert, Colin Barber, who had established himself in the States as a mathematical physicist. As a result, in 1964, a joint company was set up called Rocappi Ltd, the partners being Hazell-Sun, Westerham Press and Rocappi Inc. Barber was persuaded to return to Britain to lead the technical side of the new company.

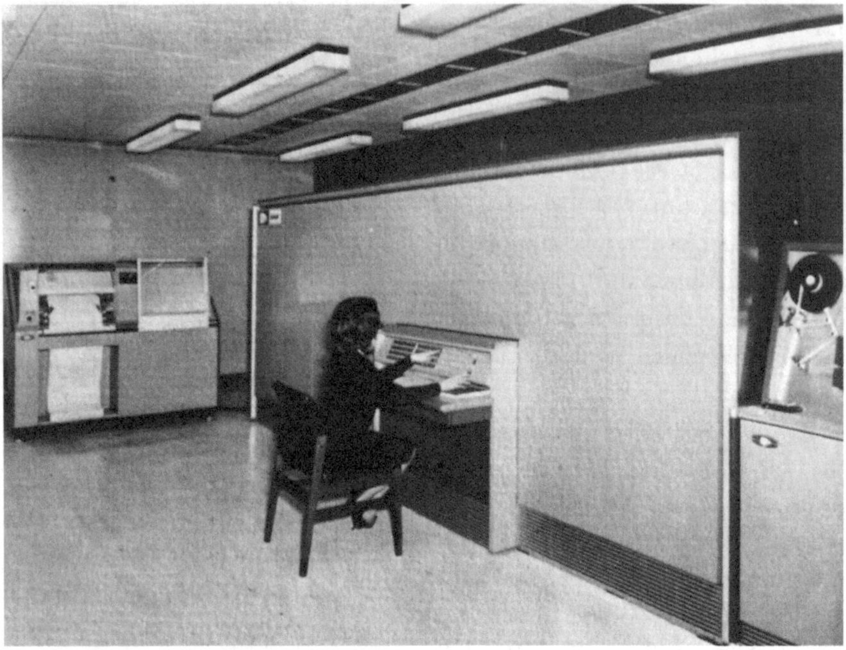

The Computer Room at Westerham Press.

Initially housed in Stratton House, Westerham, it moved to larger premises five miles away in Otford, when an ICT 1500 computer was acquired and installed. Rocappi Ltd was now up and running.

In early 1965, the first major milestone was achieved when the paper tape for a catalogue for the Worshipful Company of Goldsmiths was prepared for monotype by Rocappi UK and set in Gill Sans type by the Westerham Press film setter. They were now worldwide pioneers in the development of computer typesetting. Shortly after, Margaret Drabble's *The Millstone* was the first novel set by computer (another first was the Bible, which was first computer set by Rocappi in 1966).

Despite these early technical achievements, LMS became impatient. It was used to making a quick buck on property deals and did not understand the long lead-in time required by new technology. In December 1966, Brian Bonfield, the LMS finance director, decided that there was no future in computer typesetting and handed Westerham Press's shares in Rocappi to the British Printing Corporation (formerly Hazell-Sun).

Development costs to finance Rocappi had been lent by LMS to Westerham Press and not Rocappi. So, by way of settlement, LMS took Atterbury's 90 per cent shareholding in Westerham Press. Atterbury continued as managing director, but lost control of his company and was rendered virtually bankrupt.

Quite what Rayne thought about Bonfield's ruthless and short-sighted action is not recorded, but Bonfield was sacked not long after. Westerham Press was fully owned by LMS until 1972, when Rayne generously allowed Atterbury to buy back his company on favourable terms. However, there was one crucial consequence of Westerham's sixteen-year association with LMS – a factory. Rayne, principally a property developer, had envisaged from the start that building a new factory would be an investment, if nothing else. So, a plot covering 40,000ft was acquired next to the old Westerham railway station. A new factory was built, where all the printing processes, from design and origination to finishing, could be carried out under one roof in an environment enhanced by air conditioning and humidity controls. It made possible the production of high-quality, low-cost colour printing in one machine pass – this was unique in the printing industry at this time.

Their factory, which opened in December 1965, was the envy of the whole printing industry in the UK, which was still largely operating from premises that Charles Dickens would have recognised. With a factory, computer

The new factory next to the Old Westerham railway station in December 1965.

typesetting and a team of dedicated and talented craftsman, Westerham embarked on what was its golden decade from the late 1960s. Technologically way ahead, and with 'the pursuit of excellence' as a slogan, it soon became one of the finest colour printers in Europe.

Westerham's clients included the Tate Gallery, the Victoria & Albert Museum, the Natural History Museum, the National Portrait Gallery, Los Angeles County Museum and the Smithsonian Institute in Washington. Exports and foreign language printing were an important part of Westerham's service. Books and catalogues in the fine art category were produced for clients in the USA, Nigeria, Greece, Russia, Sweden, Saudi Arabia and elsewhere. Designers and photographers of international reputation worked with Westerham, supplementing its in-house facility. Crucially, Westerham started printing company annual reports as they increasingly became high-quality public relations documents.

This golden era was not to last. By the end of the 1970s, the chill winds of economic recession began to be felt, and print unions were making impossible demands. Universally, arts and publishing budgets were cut as the realities of the economic downturn took hold and printers' profit margins had to be cut.

Westerham, for all its technical excellence, was weak managerially. Management was a skill that Rowley Atterbury simply did not recognise, and his own laissez-faire attitude meant that Westerham Press was in no way equipped to deal with the economic vicissitudes of that era and it made a loss of nearly £200,000 in 1978–79.

And yet the print unions had in that year been awarded an extra week's paid holiday (making five weeks in all), a cut in weekly hours from thirty-seven hours and thirty minutes to thirty-five hours for the same pay, and the promise of a company pension scheme for the whole workforce of nearly 200 employees. Rowley's response to the downturn was to keep the factory ticking over with loss-making work.

Inevitably, cashflow problems became acute and the banks refused to advance any more money. Rowley was forced to talk to a leading City of London printer about a possible takeover. The situation was desperate.

However, on the advice of a well-respected printing industry figure, Ivan Heath, Rowley approached a chartered accountant, Malcolm Horton, who had a successful record of management within the printing industry. He agreed to take up the challenge of rescuing Westerham. Horton decided that the market

High-quality annual reports were a market expansion that saved Westerham, for a while.

that would produce the speediest results was the lucrative company annual reports market, which at this time was free from economic restraint, as public companies vied with one another to produce the glossiest and most eye-catching annual report.

The one obvious sales pitch was, 'Get Europe's finest colour printer to produce your glossy annual report'. A specialist salesforce was quickly recruited from London's City Printers, and within a year, sales in this market were increased by more than £1 million.

In addition, Westerham's lead in computer typesetting meant it was ideally placed to undertake City of London financial printing – takeover documents – which involved much complicated and rapidly changing typesetting. Hanson Trust became the first of many annual accounts customers who entrusted their takeover printing to Westerham Press.

During this time, two new Heidelberg Speedmasters were acquired at £250,000 each. They were four-colour machines, and one had the ability to print two colours on both sides simultaneously – ideal for the annual reports market. The machines were partly financed by a loan from a local building society because the banks had reached, and indeed exceeded, their lending limits. By the end of 1981, Westerham Press was restored to profitability.

However, the annual reports market was seasonal – most public companies end their financial year on 31 December or 31 March – so more work was needed to fill the July–December period. A superb opportunity arose in 1982 when Curwen Press approached Westerham's managing director, Malcolm

Horton, to see whether he would consider switching to them. The answer was no, but instead he asked, 'Why not consider a merger with Westerham?'

Curwen readily agreed on the basis that it would be able to shut its east London factory and transfer all work to Westerham, both companies being managed by Westerham's team. Curwen had some impressive and profitable customers in the fine art field and so an ideal balance would be struck between annual reports and art, the quieter periods assured of a steady workflow.

Was this a marriage made in heaven? Maybe, but we will never know because Atterbury, still the major shareholder, rejected the deal on the basis that he did not want to water down his independence. As a result, Malcolm Horton resigned, along with most of the specialist sales force.

Within two years, Westerham's plight became so desperate that Rowley was forced to sell the company for £100,000 to a competitor, who immediately closed the factory, with the loss of 150 jobs, and sold the factory site for £1.6 million for housing development. The town lost its major employer.

In his memoir *A Good Idea at the Time?*, published in 2010, a year before his death, Rowley Atterbury blamed the money men and the greedy print unions for Westerham's demise. This was partly true, but much of the blame must fall on Rowley. His Achilles heel – poor management skills – prevailed in the end. He was a flawed genius whose seminal influence in the printing industry was greater than his achievements. He was, arguably, the most influential figure in the British printing industry since William Caxton, 500 years before.